MULTILINGUAL BRITAIN
the educational challenge

Centre for Information on Language Teaching and Research

The views and opinions expressed in this publicaton are those of the
author and do not necessarily represent those of CILT.

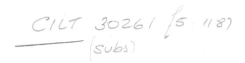

First published 1987
© 1987 Centre for Information on Language Teaching and Research
ISBN 0 948003 76 6

Printed in Great Britain by Warwick Printing Co. Ltd.

Published by Centre for Information on Language Teaching and
Research, Regent's College, Inner Circle, Regent's Park, London NW1
4NS

Contents

44/45 46/47 52/53 54/55 ,

Foreword

The title of this book indicates a significant change in perspective in thinking about educational provision in this country. It neither focusses on personal and individual bilingualism, nor only on establishing the common needs of all children through a common curriculum. Instead, it is a recognition and acceptance of the multilingual nature of British society, and the challenge this diversity, once exposed, poses to long established monolingual educational traditions.

Michael Marland's introductory chapter, "Towards a curriculum policy for a multilingual world", sets out to clarify the implications of multilingualism for the whole curriculum. As a curriculum specialist, he is well able to face and explore the implications of a multilingual society for the modern languages curriculum. However, as the headteacher of a large urban comprehensive school, he is also able to situate the argument for curriculum change within a whole school languages policy, not forgetting the implications for the hidden curriculum, nor for the practicalities of staffing and resourcing new initiatives.

As well as writing for local authority policy makers, planners, heads, teachers and student teachers, all of whom would find this book readily accessible, the plan for action which Michael Marland lays out has important implications for those involved in teacher preparation and higher education. Within his ten-point plan to move forward, eight points indicate the need for teachers of, or fluent in, the appropriate languages to be introduced into the school curriculum. The two remaining points require the availability of competent translators. While schools can make a good start towards implementing the plans by drawing on available competence among pupils and parents, and within the community, there is a pressing need for more bilingual teachers in all subject areas, and particularly for those trained as language teachers.

A national survey of teacher training institutions in 1983 (Craft and Atkins) revealed that there was no postgraduate teacher training course available for graduates in any South Asian language, and only one appropriate B.Ed. course! Moreover, scarcely any exisiting staff were identified in training institutions across the country who would be able to staff a future teacher training course. Four years later, the present position is scarcely more appropriate to the need, but a few courses have been initiated, and more are at the planning stage, indicating that the will to innovate is of greater importance than the existence of readily identified resources, and that changes are made in response to the demands of schools and communities. However, if plans such as those laid out in this book are to become a reality for more than a handful of schools, more pressure will be needed for forward planning in the recruitment and, where necessary, appropriate training of teachers from linguistic minority groups.

In the second paper included in this book, a working group of committed and experienced teachers begin to think through at the school level an appropriate and pragmatic educational response to multilingualism in the form of "a coherent overall policy of bilingual education which will inform our practical planning". Their starting point is neither the personal social adjustment of individual pupils, nor wider socio-political change, but impeccably educational: "the role of language in the educational development of children", alongside the recognition that for many children the dominant language of the family will be one other than English. Studies of the ways in which the British educational system has been responding to changing perceptions of the needs of bilingual pupils in schools over the past twenty years have uniformly commented on the lack of a central lead in policy. While there have been general trends, such as an almost exclusive concentration on provision of E2L teaching in the 1960s and '70s, there has been, and remains, wide variation in the scale and organisation of provision within local education authorities (Townsend & Brittan, 1972; Young & Connelly, 1981; Little & Willey, 1983). An ongoing study of six LEAs by the NFER "Educational Provision for Bilingual Pupils Project" suggests an increasing trend towards the provision of bilingual classroom support in the early years and of option classes in the languages spoken by local communites at 14+. There is also some smaller scale bilingual support and language maintenance work in the middle years, despite the disappointment of the (1985) Swann Report's failure to recommend provision in this area. In addition, we have found the occasional "language taster" programme for all children, which includes languages shared within some local communities.

The picture of provision overall appears patchy and ad hoc, supporting the LMP (1983) conclusion that "very few teaching schemes have been carefully planned or systematically evaluated. Initiatives within local authorities are too often hastily established, in response to pressure from local minorities or through political expediency, rather than based on sound educational principle"(p.19).

Alongside these approaches to developing languages programmes that take into account the linguistic skills of pupils, there are also strong indications that whole school policies on language(s) across the curriculum are being reassessed and that LEAs and schools are continuing, as Little and Willey (1983) expressed it, "the difficult process of adapting a pattern or organisational arrangements established to meet particular needs .... to the wider task of fulfilling the educational needs of all children in a multi-ethnic society." This is particularly seen in the rapid changes being made in patterns of organisation for English language support, in line with the Swann Report's recommendations for a change from the provision of E2L by withdrawal into language centres and units towards meeting the needs of pupils learning English as a second language "within the mainstream school as part of a comprehensive programme of language education for all children" (Swann, p.771).

Again, however, provision varies widely, both in terms of the numbers of support teachers allocated to schools, the status and expertise of these teachers, and their deployment across the school. The DES/University of London Institute of Education Project on the Initial Training of Teachers of English as a Second Language in England (Bourne, 1987) found that the schools that student teachers were placed in were offering English language support in a range of different ways, including short bilingual reception courses; timetabled withdrawal classes; more short term and flexible withdrawal groupings; support for individual pupils in subject classes in specific departments; support linked to tutor groups, with the support teacher following the group through their timetable; team teaching strategies involving language support and subject teachers taking joint responsibility for planning and teaching subject lessons; and most often in a combination of these ways.

In some schools, language support teachers were also expected to take an inservice role, helping to coordinate whole school working groups on language issues; while in other schools, language support teachers appeared to be marginalised, with little status in the school, including a number in scale 1 and probationary posts, supported by a number of supply teachers.

As Swann has pointed out with reference to the whole field of "multicultural education", most of the important initiatives in the development of language policy in this area have come from the commitment and efforts of individuals and groups, such as the joint authors of this book. Unfortunately, in the past these initiatives have rarely been shared, so that variation in provision seems as wide within local authorities as between them. In general, as Swann pointed out (p.222), changes in organisational structure have been based less on principle than on "ad hoc 'emergency' and 'compensatory' measures".

There are clear indications that the present largely ad hoc arrangements are no longer to be considered satisfactory. There has been over the past few years increasing recognition of ongoing pressure from minority ethnic groups for provision to be made both more effective and accountable. This pressure on local authorities and schools is being channelled through an unexpected quarter, the Home Office. Section 11 of the Local Government Act 1966 (Home Office Circular 72/86) is largely drawn on to fund E2L provision in the country, and until recently, new posts in "community languages" teaching.

New criteria for the use of Section 11 funding, drawn up in consultation with minority ethnic groups, require LEAs to set up procedures for monitoring the "effectiveness" of their use of Section 11 funding. Another more recent Home Office report ("The Bangladeshis in Britain" Home Affairs Committee Report, December 1986) reiterated and reinforced demands on LEAs to monitor and report back centrally on the effectiveness of their E2L provision.

However, although continuing Section 11 funding for E2L work is expected, no formulas have been suggested for staffing ratios according to needs, a point Michael Marland takes up and expands on. Changes in the organisation of E2L provision towards mainstream English language support require reappraisal of staffing needs. The role of the language support teacher requires careful examination. Once establshed, there needs to be an examination of the number of language support staff necessary to fulfil their role effectively and the type of managerial support structure necessary for them to work within in order to bring about whole school curriculum development. There will of course be implications for the consequent planning, staffing and organisation of appropriate courses of initial and inservice teacher training.

However, if English language support work is to be seen as only part of a wider strategy for reflecting and developing the multilingual nature of our society, there is a need for a comprehensive and unified policy on languages. This need has been made more urgent by recent changes in criteria for Section 11 funding. Whilst provision for teaching of the languages shared by many in the community appears again to have largely rested in the past on Section 11 funding, new interpretations of Section 11 by the Home Office may curtail its expansion by the withdrawal of central funds, unless such teaching is seen as part of the mainstream curriculum to be covered by the mainstream budget.

Section 11 funding will be provided, it seems, for bilingual support work for personal and affective reasons, or for access to the subject curriculum, but not for option classes leading to examinations in the secondary school. In itself, the Home Office argument is reasonable; such classes are mainstream modern languages classes, and therefore should be funded out of mainstream educational budgets. This will require mainstream budgets to be strictly reappraised if they are to be reapportioned in such a way as to allow for the introduction of more or different languages into the curriculum. In the present economic and political climate, there is little hope for additional funding if such provision is seen as an "optional extra". There will need to be sustained pressure to ensure that in any discussion of "a national language curriculum" there is clear recognition of the implications of multilingualism for language teaching in our society. It is by such recognition that we should judge the outcome of the Committee of

Inquiry into "English Language Teaching" (the Kingman Committee), in order that the other languages of England are not marginalised, nor bilingual skills ignored, once again, and the current piecemeal but encouraging local initiatives lost in a national curriculum.

Equally, the implications of other national policy statements need to be examined in the light of their possible effects on provision of education for bilingual pupils. For example, what might the effects be on the flexible provision of centrally based languages support team structures, such as those described by Marland, of the transferrance of powers for allocating educational funding from local authorities to individual schools?

It is in this context of politically-charged educational debate that this book makes its appearance. It offers an explicit, flexible, and readily understandable programme for action. Many of its proposals will, however, be found controversial. Covering such a wide field as languages in the context of learning across the curriculum, there are bound to be areas where those coming from different backgrounds with different perspectives will disagree, both on structural and procedural suggestions. But a major contribution of the book will be in making the implications of different ways of perceiving needs and making provision explicit. This book brings into the open discussions about the structural and procedural changes required in responding to multilingualism (discussions which are quietly taking place all over the country in staffrooms and inservice centres), and argues the case for change explicitly, identifying some constraints. By offering an explicit argument, educational decision-making becomes more accountable to society.

This book should be seen as a beginning, the start of a continuing discussion on appropriate educational provision by schools in multilingual Britain. By its nature and its outlet, it is likely to be a book mainly read by professionals; but in the discussions taking place around it, the central role of minority groups themselves in defining their own needs and perceptions of appropriate provision should not be forgotten. The original working party involved in 1985 in thinking through and writing up the discussion paper stressed the need for local minority groups to be involved in a process of consultation, criticism and constructive feedback. The discussion has already been long delayed. It would be a great pity if participation in that debate should now also be limited.

Tom Gorman/Jill Bourne
NFER, June 1987

Preface

This book is about the education response to one of the greatest changes in British life - the move to a multilingual society. Generally the newly arrived languages, which can now properly be labelled by The Linguistic Minorities Project as 'the other languages of England', have regrettably been seen only as a transitory 'problem'. Despite hard work by individual schools and teachers, the education system at all levels, from the DES to the class teacher, has been slow to respond even in areas where there is already a substantial linguistic minority population in the schools - and the monolingual anglophone areas have rarely considered the issue.

The first section of the book is the revised text of a paper originally prepared for a far-seeing conference organised by the London Borough of Newham on the teaching of South Asian languages, and I am grateful to the then Director of Education, James Pailing, and Dr Manju Aggerwal for prompting me into preparing it. I subsequently revised it for the annual conference of the Joint Council of Language Associations, and it was printed in that version in The British Journal of Language Teaching (vol. 24, No.3). I am grateful to the Editor for permission to include this version here.

The second part of the book is an edited version of the report, probably unique in the country, of a working party in the Camden and Westminster division of the ILEA which met over a period of eighteen months to study the needs of the bilingual learners. The membership of the group (set out on page 31) brought together teachers, administrators, and community representatives to endeavour to work towards a policy. The working party was very grateful to its secretary, Alison Leake, who was invaluable in preparing the text. She has now produced a specially edited version, which takes out all specific ILEA references but retains the general arguments, that we hope will be useful as a help to the discussion of others in many parts of the country. I am grateful to the members of the Working Party and the Education Officers for their willingness to support the publication of this new version.

Finally I have produced a bibliography, which not only acts as a list of all references in the texts of the two parts of the book, but also is offered as a starting point for those who want to consider the issues more fully themselves.

Many of the difficulties in education come from a lack of resources, weakness of organisation, or our having insufficient skills. I believe, however, that there is a deeper problem in meeting the needs of a multilingual world: we simply have not done the thinking either on the needs of bilingual learners or on the gains for and the needs of monolingual anglophones. Without a conceptual exploration we shall never develop policies and not be in a position intelligently to seek the appropriate resources.

Not only do the bilingual learners of this country require this thinking, the development of suitable policies, and the provision of necessary resources, but the whole place of languages in education has to be re-thought. The presence of bilingual learners is a potential richness for the future cultural, intellectual, commercial, and political life of the country. We shall miss a rich opportunity if we do not urgently develop an education response.

Michael Marland

The preparation of the final text, the editing, and the word-processing were made possible by a grant from the Education and Human Development Committee of the Economic and Social Research Council.

Towards a curriculum policy for a multilingual world

Michael Marland, C.B.E., M.A.

Headteacher, North Westminster Community School, ILEA
Honorary Professor of Education, Warwick University

INTRODUCTION

World-wide bilingualism is not only not strange; it is indeed normal. Some seventy percent of the world population is bilingual. Yet the British education system has been led by monolingual Anglophones, professionals who have themselves been well served in most respects by similarly monolingual education systems, and in their turn have, naturally perhaps, created a curriculum, pastoral care, and administrative structure that is linguistically firmly Anglo-centric. (The frequent Francophile could be seen, in a curious way, as actually strengthening this linguistic close-focus.)

It is almost as if many of us have forgotten one of the most common reminders in western culture of multi-lingualism, the gospel climax:

> And there they crucified Him, and two others with Him, on either side one, and Jesus in the midst. And Pilate wrote a title, and put it on the cross. And the writing was, Jesus of Nazareth, the King of the Jews. This title then read many of the Jews, for the place was nigh to the city where Jesus was crucified, and it was written in Hebrew, and Greek, and Latin.

John 19:20

Indeed we have more substantial experiences of bilingualism in the United Kingdom than is usually accounted for. Not only do we have strong examples from the Celtic areas, but we should not forget what a recent writer called this period of bilingualism (Burchfield, 1985, p.14):

> In 1066 the Normans came and more or less transformed English and also the way it was written down. From then for nearly three hundred years the official language was French, though English remained the ordinary language of the majority of the population.

(ibid.)

Even later than that there were lingering traces of a wider approach to languages than we know. Indeed the study of grammar in the seventeenth century 'was a multilingual exercise' (Burchfield, 1985, p.94). John Brinsley in 1612 spoke of the study as 'to write fayre in Secretary, Romane, Greeke, Hebrue' and 'to know all the principal necessary Radicis, Greeke and Hebrue' (cited ibid). Such was, however, not a popular view in the nineteenth century, and the unprecedented spread of English as a world-wide language has not only brought income to our educational, cultural, and publishing activities, but allowed us to overlook our needs to consider education for a multilingual world. The sharply increased immigration to the UK of people whose first or strongest language is other than English must force us to change our perspective. As Burchfield says generally:

Historical events usually have linguistic as well as
political and social results.

(Burchfield, 1985, p.11)

And the linguistic results are clearly detailed in the powerfully
but simply titled research report <u>The Other Languages of England</u>
(Linguistic Minorities Project, 1985). This shows that to be
English is no longer necessarily to have English as one's first or
strongest language. The figures are startling to some, even
frightening for others, but are worth pondering for all of us in
their implications for the curriculum: for instance, in 1981 the
proportions of bilingual pupils in five LEAs was:

Bradford	:	17.8%
Coventry	:	14.4%
Haringey	:	30.7%
Peterborough	:	7.4%
Waltham Forest	:	18.8%

(Linguistic Minorities, 1985, p.336)

This article is a consideration of the implications of our pupils'
bilingualism and the bilingualism of much of the world and the great
urban centres of our country for the curriculum. I consider what I
take to be the five major problems first, for without analysing
those we cannot face them and thus hope to change the curriculum. I
then attempt to outline ten points towards a coherent programme for
a multilingual curriculum.

*   *   *   *   *

A   FIVE MAJOR PROBLEMS

In considering languages in schools I perceive five major problems,
each interlinking and some being deep, attitudinal ones.

1   The conspiracy of deafness

'The Tower of Babel' is a powerful metaphor, embedded deep in the
sub-consciousness of those of us who are monolingual Anglophones and
for whom since the Norman Conquest, 'Englishness' has been primarily
expressed by speaking 'English'. The myth of the Tower of Babel was
outlined by Hobbes, and many Christians accepted the formulation in
his influential <u>Leviathan</u>:

4

> All this language gotten and augmented by Adam and his posterity, was again lost at the Tower of Babel, when by the hand of God, every man was stricken for his rebellion, with an oblivion of his former language.
> (Thomas Hobbes, 1651, I.VI.12)

This view is still that unconsciously or consciously held by many and even taught by some. One summer recently I went to a leaving service for a group of Church of England primary schools. The overall theme, to which each school's eleven-year-old class contributed, was: 'We are all one world'. One school chose to feature the biblical story of the Tower of Babel. As interpreted, vividly and skilfully, the myth taught that humanity behaved badly, and as a punishment for error God cursed people, and ruined their ability to work together by imposing a baffling range of languages. This message was being vividly portrayed to young children under the bland hope of 'We are all one world'.

I suggest that the first problem faced by those really considering a curriculum policy for languages is the fear of the multilingual world, which leads to a 'conspiracy of deafness'. The United Kingdom appears to be trying to ignore the existence of bilingualism. The Swann Report is right to talk about linguistic prejudice (Committee of Enquiry, 1985, Chapter 7, paragraph 1.3). Indeed, in the educational debate in British society generally there is what could be accurately regarded as a conspiracy of silence about what the Linguistic Minorities Project appropriately call, 'The Other Languages of England' (L.M.P., 1985). The numerically and politically dominant monolingual Anglophones ensure that the verbal and written public life of the country excludes the reality of its actual multilingualism. The school system simply has not been led to consider the curriculum implications of our multilingual society or the wider multilingual world.

Indeed, to many of us who eccentrically speak only English the ability to speak another language fluently, especially if it is a 'first' or 'home' language, is a serious and sad 'problem', requiring sympathy. School staff talk about "How many 'EEE-Too'Ells' (E2Ls) have you got?" or even say, as I have heard: "We've got some very eetooells". The fact that the linguistic diversity that lies behind those prejudicial phrases is a great educational potential is masked by so many people's refusal to hear the bilingualism of our society, and the overwhelming fear of the problems it all causes in a world that would be so simple if humanity hadn't called the curse of 'Babel' down from God. Languages other than English are evaluated as of low status, especially if of ways of life historically and culturally remote from Europe, as those of Asia.

Many pupils suffer from racism as a result of the way people perceive their ethnicity. For many this denigration is amplified by a widespread low evaluation of the languages they speak. These pupils go to school with keen parental encouragement and high hopes. The school then reveals itself as a place where all the adults speak a foreign language, English. Other languages appear officially not to exist, apart from sadly ineffective lessons called 'Modern Languages', (actually French). These pupils are already clearly disadvantaged by their income and class and by the racism of others, and for them English is obviously and strenuously the language of an alien culture, the well regarded, the financially well off - of all those with effective power. I saw in Boston, USA, amongst the Hispanic community, soon to become the largest minority, a pattern analogous to that, for instance, of the Bangladeshi population in London: speaking a lower-status language is as discriminatory a target as having a lower-status skin colour (MacDonald et al., 1982). This linguistic aspect of racism has not been properly explored, even by the anti-racist writers. We have created a kind of linguistic parochialism which prevents us from seeing the rich offering our bilingual pupils bring to our curriculum planning or the needs for linguistic understanding of our currently monolingual Anglophone pupils. Compare this with how we treat other skills pupils bring with them to school: if a pupil is good at games or music she or he is encouraged to demonstrate these skills and appropriately praised. The fact that a pupil comes to us expert at a language other than English is seen as a 'problem', not normally as a matter for congratulation, and certainly not that she or he has a skill to share with other pupils.

As long ago as 1975 The Bullock Report spoke against this attitude, stressing in a now-famous phrase that:

> No child should be expected to cast off the language and culture of the home as he crosses the school threshold, and the curriculum should reflect those of his life.
> (Committee of Enquiry, Rec.249, p.543)

More specifically it stated:

> Their bilingualism is of great importance to the children and their families, and also to society as a whole. In a linguistically conscious nation in the modern world we should see it as an asset, as something to be nurtured, and one of the agencies that should nurture it is the school. Certainly the school should adopt a positive attitude towards its pupils' bilingualism and wherever possible should help maintain and deepen their knowledge of their mother tongues.
> (Committee of Enquiry, 1975, p.294)

The words 'and deepen' need stressing - they are far from the

6

limited sense of the Swann use of 'maintenance' (Committee of Enquiry, 1985, Chapter 7).

In a linguistically conscious nation we should see it as an asset and something to be nurtured that our pupils bring a variety of languages to school with them. Schools should adopt a positive attitude towards their pupils' bilingualism and ensure that they develop and deepen their knowledge - and use it to widen and enrich the languages curriculum.

The Swann report is not deaf to the world's true linguistic pattern. Early in Chapter 7 it gets the general aim right.

> In order to lay the foundations for a genuinely pluralist society the education system must, we believe, both cater for the linguistic needs of ethnic minority pupils and also take full advantage of the opportunities offered for the education of all pupils by the linguistic diversity of our society today.   (Chapter 7, 1.1., p.385)

The spirit is not, however, representative of our world, and in much multicultural education the linguistic component is left out. In most surveys of multicultural education the languages element is under-emphasised. Indeed, schools attempting to develop a multicultural curriculum in which the ethnocentricity of the previous curriculum and learning materials is challenged are usually surprisingly slow to respond to linguistic diversity. There are many secondary schools in which Humanities and English Departments are busy revealing a range of cultural patterns and literature, but where monolithic French is the languages curriculum, from the verb 'to be' in the first week of September until they slip back to 'European Studies' when they have finally 'failed' at French. New initiatives in the curriculum have usually left the languages policy of school untouched.

Indeed the 'deafness' even extends to libraries in schools with a large proportion of bilingual pupils. In one junior school, in which some seventy percent of the children had the same Indian language as the home language, a key researcher found 'no books in other languages (except French) were allowed, least of all the dominant language of the school - "otherwise they wouldn't read English"' (Klein, 1985, p.19). A less crass but equally powerful result of the 'deafness' is to segregate books in or on languages other than European. The same researcher, for instance, reports of a secondary school with a fifty percent Asian population that books in 'community languages are all in the "E2L room"' (op. cit., p.33).

The publication of The Other Languages of England (L.M.P., 1985) can be taken as the first public sign-posting that to be 'English' is not necessarily to speak English as your strongest or first

7

language. While, though, so many stalwartly refuse to face the
linguistic facts of life, schools are inevitably given problems in
planning an appropriate languages response to real life needs and
pleasures.

2   A distaste for distant language

A specially strong part of that refusal to hear, or abhorrence of
having to hear, is the dislike, to an extent which I think is real
distaste, of languages felt to be distant. Thus we especially
undervalue non-European languages. If I am right, the resolutely
monolingual ear and voice of this country is made the more
prejudicial by the deeply if vaguely held attitude that languages
(all regrettably, mind you) can be listed in an order of reluctant
acceptability, with our nearest neighbour, French, first; the
practical but 'not attractive' German second; Russian politically
important; Spanish, the flippant uncultural language of package
tours, next; and South Asian languages way beyond the pale. Lest
readers might think that I am being far-fetched, I need to remind us
that a recent Secretary of State for Education was capable of
authorising a key government document (A Frame-work for the
Curriculum) which had the biggest give-away of our time: it used
the phrases 'European languages' and 'modern languages' synonymously
(DES, 1980, p.7)! In the ears and mind of the then educational
leader there were no 'modern' languages outside Europe! And many
school libraries would be a clear embodiment of this attitude.

There are, of course, sociolinguistic and other intellectual
problems about my use of the phrase 'distant' languages. However, I
am sure there is a real feeling of 'distance', an alienation
measure. It is only partly cultural (e.g. Poland has a cultural
link which Yugoslavia has not), and partly linguistic (e.g. non-
Roman scripts frighten us).

This is confirmed by official documents on education. The then
powerful Schools Council's Modern Languages Committee, for instance,
used the phrase 'second foreign languages' to mean one of German,
Spanish, Italian, and Russian. Its Eurocentric focus was clearly
stated when it justified this 'second foreign language' solely in
terms of 'our political and economic development in Europe' (Schools
Council Modern Languages Committee, 1982, p.13). A year later the
DES itself in a consultatie document on Foreign Languages in the
School Curriculum devoted only some 22 lines to what it called
'languages of Minority Communities'. It simplistically noted that
'among the questions to be considered are ... the scope for making
ethnic community languages available as a curriculum option' (DES,
1983, p.11). How can great and widely spoken languages of the world
be dubbed only as 'languages of minority communities'? Even those
in the forefront of urging the teaching of Asian languages in

8

schools have usually limited their arguments to the fact that these
languages are local community languages (e.g. an otherwise powerful
piece by Srivastava, 1982)! The final indictment is that Sir James
Craig's enquiry for the University Grants Committee on the teaching
of non-European languages at universities has a brief that does not
allow a consideration of schools: yet there is no future for non-
European languages at universities without a foundation in the
schools. The dominance of French is a clear indication of our
linguistic myopia.

This 'distaste of distance' unbelievably surfaces in the Swann
report. Surely that Committee was wrong to argue that 'the major
argument for broadening the modern languages curriculum to include
ethnic minority languages is that it is sound educational practice,
as well as common sense, for pupils to study for and obtain a
qualification in a language in which they may already have some
facility' (Committee of Enquiry, 1984, p.400). That is one
argument, but it is an inadequate basis for curriculum planning.
Indeed, its logic suggests that if a school has no pupils, say, who
have any previous facility in French or Physics, those subjects
should be taken off the curriculum!

This Swann argument is a startling anti-educational way of thinking.
There is no mention in Swann that an Asian language (or Arabic) or
course, not arguing that local use is not an argument for
considering a language, but that this is not and cannot be a sole
argument. I should wish to argue that languages are taught because
they are worth learning, they have a claim on the curriculum, and
the country needs speakers of these languages. Arabic, Hindi, Urdu,
for instance, need considering as much as Italian, French, Spanish,
or German. Only our 'distaste of distance' puts us off.

3   **Reluctance to teach the mother tongue**

The third problem is the widespread reluctance to teach in or
through the mother tongue, a phrase which I am using deliberately
for this part. (I shall not keep debating between the phrases
'heritage', 'community', and 'mother tongue', but I think the last
is more appropriate for this section.) There is a deep-seated
belief that to learn the language of your home is definitely going
to confuse you. The international evidence is very substantial and
wide-ranging that it does not (e.g. Dodson, 1985). Yet, I sense
that very many parents, governors, and teachers have a 'common-
sense' worry that learning English is hampered by developing the
'conflicting' mother tongue.

There is also a straightforward control fear of pupils communicating
in a language the teacher does not understand: what may they be
getting up to? This is a genuine teacherly fear, both in the

9

classroom and on playground or corridor supervision. 'If I don't understand what those two are saying they may be making fun of me!'

Then, of course, there is the oft-quoted worry about resource implications. Yet in, for instance, Toronto, and in the USA under the Lau remedies (Lau, 1974), there are automatically applied formulae. Here we create problems with more ingenuity than we solve them. In most areas the dominant minority languages are present in sufficient numbers for easy organisation. With small-representation languages (e.g. the Division in ILEA in which I teach has only a little over one hundred Tagalog speakers) cross-area provision is required. Even so, the fact that something cannot be done completely should not prevent as much as possible from being carried out. (Cf., A level chemistry for small-number schools in the ILEA, for which a centrally prepared teaching resource, Apel, was produced.)

No wonder that until recently there has been very little teaching of mother tongue (never mind through), and even now it is marginal and patchy. As the Centre for Information on Language Teaching and Research observed as long ago as 1976, there are 'in Britain and particularly in England ... many thousands of bilingual children whose mother tongues are largely ignored educationally" (CILT, 1976, p.7). Indeed, the majority of the teaching profession and many members of the public still bring their English-centric attitudes to bear, and further argue that retaining and developing the mother tongue confuses the pupil and impedes the learning of English. The EEC Directive of 1977 (EEC., 1977; and cf. the commentary in Commission for Racial Equality, 1980) has hardly impinged, and the DES circular to implement it was not issued until July 31, 1981 (DES 1981), six days after all Member States should have complied! Unlike, for instance, Belgium, Bavaria, France, or Denmark, the UK has not followed this Directive by establishing the number of pupils concerned (Commission of the European Communities, 1984, p. UK.1), and the DES states that 'it is impossible to give a comprehensive summary of the measures taken to receive pupils whose mother tongue is not English' (op. cit., p. UK.2)! No wonder that the comments by the Commission are tart, especially criticising the fact that 'even according to the most favourable estimates integrated tuition in the language and culture of origin is offered to only 2.2% of pupils whose first language is not English' (op. cit., p. UK.6).

In my view the Swann Committee Report makes matters worse in its distinction (Committee of Enquiry, 1984, para. 3.4 of Chapter 7) between 'Mother Tongue Teaching' and 'Mother Tongue Maintenance'. You cannot 'maintain' a language in pupils, as if it were a washing machine: without 'teaching' and 'development' it must fade and deteriorate (cf. Khan, 1985).

There is then a frequently displayed fear that bilingual education teaching promotes separatism. In fact there is a whole panic, derived understandably from past UK traditions of discrimination via separation (e.g. selective schooling, language centres, remedial streams). Thus, within the formal school week any form of special group is frowned on (even to the extent of arguing as if no recently arrived bilingual pupils requiring English started secondary schools!), but mother-tongue work is relegated to out of school.

We would regard mother tongue maintenance, although an important educational function, as best achieved within the ethnic minority communities themselves rather than within mainstream schools, but with considerable support from and liaison with the latter.
(Committee of Enquiry, 1984, p.406)

Although the former Secretary of State for Education had a genuine regard for the learning of languages, and pointed out that 'the acquisition of linguistic skills is a rich and fascinating field for study' (Joseph, 1984, p.3), he was really quite discouraging, as if he considered that linguistic minority communities needed protecting from the ambitions of the education system to force unwanted tuition onto families, arguing on the grounds of 'the desirable limits of state intervention', stressing that 'where the family's free choice is to maintain the language, then it is for relatives and friends and the wider community to explore the achievement of that end through voluntary and non-publically provided funds' (ibid, p.1). Despite his welcome encouragement of the creation in state schools of a 'background atmosphere within the school which encourages children to respect other cultures and to admire proficiency in more that one language' (ibid. p.2) and his admirable stressing that 'linguistic minorities need not be seen as having a problem - lack of practice in English - but as having an asset, a skill in language' (ibid. p.2), Sir Keith Joseph gave very little encouragement towards the development of mother tongues and the education of bilingual learners, and Kenneth Baker has not added any further analysis. But not for one hundred and thirty years has it been encroaching on family and community life to offer desirable education in schools! The series of half-formed arguments brought forward to keep away, limit, or marginalise mother-tongue teaching mostly derives from our linguistic prejudices described in sections one and two.

4   A poor language-teaching base

The teaching of languages other than English, despite devoted and skilful work by many teachers, is surely one of the weakest aspects of our schooling. This is more than a reflection of the English attitude to foreigners. The twenty-five years of comprehensive development did not find a way of making sense of the languages aspect of the curriculum, and a mis-match developed between the inherent needs of languages teaching in learning and the dominant curriculum and classroom style ethos of the successful aspects of the comprehensive curriculum. The former inevitably is 'mastery' orientated, teacher dominated, requires audio concentration, and has limited scope for reaction and opinion. The successful subjects have, rather, been peer-group orientated, process dominated, allowing some relaxation of the quiet rule, and growing from the pupils' reactions, opinions, and sharing of experience.

National figures show a low option take-up for languages, very strong sex stereotyping, a language department standing to one side of the main stream of the school, and often too small for intellectual, organisational, or pedagogical strength. The process of the language lessons is limited by the lack of opportunity to use language. The specialist on bi-lingual education in Wales, CJ Dodson, has sharply described this central lack:

> The language itself has become the ultimate target of the learning process, and is viewed as such by teachers and pupils alike. In this environment, whether activity work takes place or not, language is not a tool to be used in the process of communicating about something which is not language.   (Dodson, 1976, p.79)

All in all I do not see the UK secondary school as having the successful and central language teaching base for an easy and vigorous approach to the needs of bilingual pupils and a multilingual world.

5   Inadequate research and policy development

Over ten years ago the Bullock Committee recommended after its brief eleven-page chapter (Committee of Enquiry, 1975, pp.284-94):

> There should be further research into the teaching of their own language to children of immigrant communities and into the various aspects of bilingualism in schools.
>   (ibid. rec. 255, p.545)

The Swann Committee regrettably has not provided that. In 1981 a key School's Council report considering multi-cultural education urged:

> ... initiation of work to assess the benefits and practical difficulties in providing (i) teaching of minority ethnic groups' languages in schools, (ii) teaching other subjects in minority ethnic groups' mother tongues, (iii) support for language teaching organised by

the minority ethnic group communities.
(Little and Willey, 1981, pp.32-34)

The DES-funded MOTET report was a helpful, but very modest study of the value of the use of mother tongues in the early curriculum (University of Bradford, 1985). The substantial survey research of the Linguistic Minorities Project (LMP, 1985) is a most valuable demonstration of the linguistic basis of our population. What was not within its brief was to work towards a policy. We have not been given the leadership by central government, the Schools Council, or even the SCDC (despite its good mother-tongue project) that the challenge requires. Although the circumstances of other countries are different from ours and precise copies of their patterns would not work, and although no doubt not all experiences elsewhere are fully successful, it is shaming that Sweden, Bavaria, Massachusetts, and Toronto, for instance, have clear policies that have statutory force, whilst we have no lead from the centre at all.

*   *   *   *   *

These five major difficulties have led to there being no coherent national or LEA policy for bilingual learners or preparing children for a multilingual society. I do not consider we have had a proper lead from the DES to help LEAs and schools evolve such a coherent policy. I would argue that virtually no schools have whole-school policies that relate to this. Even many of the very active schools which have vigorous teaching of a South Asian language make it a closely focused thing, not part of the whole-school curriculum policy. A few years ago the ILEA took a very important step in endorsing the teaching of mother tongue in Report 2321 in 1982, and recommended the appointment of an inspector for mother-tongue teaching (ILEA, 1982, p.7). The Committee approved that in 1982 and two years later in 1984 an inspector was appointed. There are 55,000 bilingual pupils in the ILEA and we have 55 bilingual teachers working for us - a pretty good ratio of one to a thousand! But even that policy document, good as it was in its way, had no formulae for mother-tongue staffing; it did not consider the key issues of some subject or content teaching being in the mother tongue; it did not consider the whole languages curriculum; and above all it did not produce a coherent overall bilingual education policy. By 'a policy', I don't mean something everybody everywhere has to do exactly, but a set of criteria to help schools make judgments.

Encouragingly we know that there is a little support for bilingualism growing up and down the country. Pauline Tansley's and

13

Alma Craft's survey in 1984 found some evidence of 'a growing network of support for bilingualism' (Tansley and Craft, 1984, p.367), and 'increasing efforts of LEAs to meet the needs of such children' (ibid., p.382). About one third of LEAs now have a policy on mother-tongue teaching, but there appears to be no evidence from the survey that even those who have developed some form of mother-tongue-teaching policy have related this to the other components (especially teaching through the mother tongue and the implications for all languages teaching) that must make up a true bilingual education policy. In particular, it is quite clear that we are all finding difficulties of coherence with E2L teaching on the one hand and other foreign-language teaching on the other hand.

*   *   *   *   *

So I want to argue that because of those five problems the educational system has not developed a philosophy for a multilingual world or for bilingual learners. The multi-cultural debate often stops short of language and teachers treat 'E2L children' as if they were a transitory problem. A policy should be based on the notion that bilingualism is a permanent and important aspect of British world life, it is a strength of the individual, and a gain for society. Modern research evidence shows that there is considerable cognitive advantage to be derived from the development of bilingual skills. The presence of bilingual pupils is and must be a gain for initially monolingual pupils, and can alter and improve the whole languages climate of a school. We cannot cope with the challenge of bilingualism by adding a few E2L teachers here and a few mother-tongue teachers there. There has to be a radical look at the whole school curriculum and the place of all languages. This will sometimes mean a differentiated curriculum.

Although continental European and North American situations are different from ours, we must learn from the more coherent approaches in many continental European countries, Australia, Canada, and the USA. Both Sweden's Directive 1981:49 and the USA's Bilingual Act of 1970 guarantee heritage-language teaching as of right. There is also a firm legislative and policy background in other countries: Canada, for instance, has had legislation since 1980, and a Minister of State for Multiculturalism. Sweden has had legislation since 1968, with frequent later improvements. For instance, since an Ordinance of 21 June 1979, children who are still monolingual in a language have a legal right to be taught their home language and be given other lessons in that language. Swedish is then successively introduced as a teaching language. In the USA, federal legislation has established the right of 'heritage language teaching' and, indeed, a full bilingual education. The historic 1974 USA Federal

14

Government Court ruling led to the essential needs of bilingual pupils being embodied in legislation. The Court ruled importantly:

> There is no equality of treatment by providing students with the same facilities, teachers and curriculum. For students who do not understand English are effectively foreclosed from a meaningful education. (Lau, 1974)

This simple but fundamental truth was expressed in legislation and then in mandatory policies. School districts and schools as a result have been able to develop coherent educational policies for bilingual pupils, which consider the pupils' overall educational experience, as well as their right to and need for mother-tongue development and when appropriate for teaching through the pupil's mother tongue. From clearly articulated aims and policies have come coherent bilingual education practices and mandatory resourcing.

The United Kingdom requires a coherent policy that will embrace bilingual learners and all pupils for a multilingual world. This will involve a more coherent whole-school policy, to which the old-established 'Modern Languages Departments' will have to contribute substantially, but which will also affect the whole school's work.

*   *   *   *   *

B   **TOWARDS A COHERENT CURRICULUM**

A coherent curriculum approach is required which has the complementary facets of preparing all pupils for a multilingual world and at the same time meeting the needs and strengths of bilingual pupils. Such a curriculum is surely going to involve relating together the teaching about people's languages in Humanities, the main non-English language teaching, the teaching of English to all, the teaching of English as a second language, the teaching of mother tongues, teaching through the mother tongues, and pastoral care. Of course, it should be tautologous to speak of a 'multilingual curriculum': as the world is multilingual, the curriculum that prepares pupils for it should be similarly multilingual. For some years ahead, though, we need to stress the word to remind ourselves of the ambition.

Here is my ten-point plan to move forward:

1   **Change attitudes**

Every way possible must be found of changing attitudes to

bilingualism and to non-European languages in particular. Although this is not easy it is probably the most important. There is a circular relationship: without changes in attitude the curriculum is less likely to change but, conversely, without a huge broadening out from our French-dominated programmes the community's attitudes will not change.

There are, though, many things a school can do: its sign system, especially the initial "welcome" sign, should be multilingual. All school publications should demonstrate a multilingual approach. For instance, at North Westminster the pupils' Diary has the message to parents in five languages. Similarly, languages other than English should be audible on public-address announcements (as in the High Schools of many Californian school boards), in assemblies, and in readings and performances. Programmes of literature can be presented bilingually. For instance in the year of preparing this paper we have at North Westminster organised the following small example:

(a) In a "personal choice" community evening, Shelley's Ozymandias was read first in English and then by a bilingual Bengali/ English teacher in a Bengali translation.

(b) In a programme of Philipino Rondalya band music played to assembly by a local young people's group, I read a poem in an English translation from the Tagalog, and then a Philipino Tagalog first-language speaker read the Tagalog original.

(c) On the occasion of a visit by the Egyptian Minister of Education to the school, he was invited to attend assembly. Egyptian poems from the Arabic were read first in English and then in Arabic by an older pupil who was learning Arabic as a foreign language.

(d) During the London celebrations of the 125th anniversary of the birth of Rabindranath Tagore an assembly was prepared with readings in English and Bengali of his poetry, with 'cross-language' performed - i.e. some obviously English first-language readers in Bengali and vice-versa, for a language is not the property of its first-language speakers and pupils should be encouraged to realise that they too have access to the literature and language of languages other than English.

(e) An evening full-length performance of Tagore's writings was similarly proposed for an audience of older students and adults.

Similarly, the library stock must be multilingual, and books in languages other than English must be integrated.

The foundation course in Humanities should find a way of featuring languages: a study of people must include a consideration of their languages. This will not usually be the occasion for 'teaching the language' (although Archbishop Michael Ramsay School in the ILEA does), but it is possible to change attitudes quite considerably.

Finally, there are many aspects of the hidden curriculum which can be subtly changed. For instance, I used to use the phrase "I'm sorry, he doesn't speak English", but now I am more likely to say "I'm sorry, I can't speak Bengali".

On a larger front, the broadcasting authorities, LEAs, and Borough Councils could do a great deal to make languages other than English more visible and audible and more natural.

2 A Languages foundation course

It should be a truism that 'French' does not equal 'languages', nor even French, German, and Spanish equal 'modern languages'. A French Department is not a 'Languages' department. It is, indeed, very difficult, if not impossible, to tack non-European languages onto the periphery of a French course. Nor, as I have argued earlier, are classes in languages such as Gujerati, Urdu, Punjabi, Hindi, Bengali, Arabic, Cantonese ... justified solely because local people speak them. Similarly, it is not only mother-tongue speakers who should learn non-European languages, nor should the mother tongue be available only as an option against a foreign language in the early years. Why shouldn't the linguistically-able bilingual English/Bengali-speaking pupil add French or Spanish as equally as Arabic or ... ?

It would be difficult to replace French as the typical first language by a single non-European language. For instance, it would neither be acceptable nor logical to replace French with, say, Urdu. However, it is possible both to broaden the languages base and to get good later success at a chosen language by giving all pupils a 'languages foundation course'.

My recommendation is for a languages foundation course which has between two and four foundation languages, as diverse as possible, which are taught in a 'through-planned' languages curriculum for, say, two years, and which incorporates what is usually now called 'Language Awareness' (c.f. Hawkins, 1984, and Marland, 1980). These units of languages other than the major foundation ones are there not only as "tasters" but also as part of the understanding of language being taught. I must stress that the languages included will very likely relate to those used by local communities, but this is not the only justification, and even in monolingual Anglophone areas the languages foundation course is highly desirable.

17

For six years now North Westminster has run such a course, and I can really say it is one of the most successful parts of the curriculum, that keeps pupils stimulated and interested, gets excellent fifth-year exam results in the later chosen languages, - and opens up the range of languages responded to by the pupils, as well as bringing into the curriculum the existing linguistic diversity and strengths of the pupils.

Certainly such a course requires teachers who can go beyond their first and second language, and certainly offers a threat to many French teachers. Indeed the reduction in the role of French in the curriculum can be psychologically threatening to many and has marked career implications. However, teachers of languages have a great deal to gain from the wider approach to language. Indeed in the experience of North Westminster the challenge of teaching the languages foundation course, with its three foundation languages and world languages project units, is linguistically, intellectually, and pedagogically stimulating for the teacher.

The series of books for pupils Awareness of Language gives a simple start to that facet of a foundation course. For instance Language Varieties and Change is an excellent lively introduction for class use (Pomphrey, 1985). However, there is currently little or no material for a foundation approach to a number of languages. I know of only a few schools carrying out such work (Camden School for Girls, Archbishop Michael Ramsay, Holland Park, and North Westminster), and each has to prepare its own material.

3   Offer more languages for examination

The figures for the domination of French in first-level examinations have worried specialists for years. Usually, though, the objectors have been fighting only to push in German, Spanish, and, much more rarely, Russian. Even in those schools that make French the single first language, why has another European language inevitably had to be the second non-English language on offer in the option years? I am arguing not in terms of "mother tongue", but in terms of the grounds of choice by a school for its second foreign language, usually chosen by those who have shown themselves to be linguistically able. Arabic (as at North Westminster), a south Asian language, or an Oriental language could well be offered. Some languages likely to be less popular should be on offer in language centres or through cooperation with the local Adult Education Institutes. In some cases classes can be shared by the L1 and L2 speakers, as has been demonstrated in Slough. This is especially so when linguistic minority pupils are not fluent or less practised in their so-called 'mother tongue' but have a knowledge ready to be activated.

North Westminster has had a fourth- and fifth-year option in Arabic (as a _foreign_ language) for a few years now, and some twenty pupils who have no family background in Arabic opt each year. This language is _not_ on the subject list because of the local Arabic-speaking communities but because of the intrinsic interest of the language and its world cultural and commercial importance.

I am also very keen to broaden the range of examined languages in a more unusual way, that is to offer a _multi-language_ GCSE examination, i.e. one in which candidates have to demonstrate some ability in three or four languages, rather than a higher standard in one. This seems to me to be perfectly academically respectable: for instance we have fifth-year examinations in 'world religions' as well as in Islam or Christianity, and we have General Science, as well as the specialised disciplines. Why, then, only single-language exams? A multi-language examination course would be useful, intellectually ambitious, and educationally exciting. To have a grounding in a number of languages would be an attractive challenge. Such a course would offer the school an opportunity to introduce non-European languages. It could well become a classic CPVE course.

A key part of the appropriate approach to the multi-lingual curriculum, then, is that quite apart from the mother-tongue/community languages arguments there should be a determined effort to offer more languages, especially including non-European languages, in examination courses in as many schools and colleges as possible.

4   In-School teaching of community languages

The arguments about under whose auspices community languages should be taught frequently become self-contradictory and confused. The Swann report in Chapter Seven allows only mother-tongue "maintenance" (Committee of Enquiry, 1985, p.406), and prefers the community to retain responsibility - though LEAs are encouraged to offer support, finance, and encouragement.

Of course, where a community wishes to and can organise its own classes, such support from the LEA is adequate - provided also that links with the state schools can be built up. However, the mainstream school system must take responsibility for ensuring that there is adequate community language-teaching provision. Sometimes this will be in a particular school for only the pupils of that school; at other times pupils will have to be drawn from many schools.

More debatable is whether the classes should be on the timetable - thus taking away some time from the rest of the curriculum. The arguments are nicely balanced: why lose another subject to retain your bilingual growth? On the other hand why put mother-tongue work for some pupils in the difficult post-school hours, when anglophones have their mother-tongue work safely in the main timetable?

I do not consider rigid positions need be taken. For instance in the primary school, community-language teaching can easily take place alongside the continuing class-teacher curriculum of the rest of the day. In the secondary option system mother-tongue languages are easily inserted - the pupil is not losing, as she or he has access to English also, which is a second language, and thus has compatibility of choice and range.

The early secondary years are more difficult: to offer, as some schools are now doing, the pupil his or her mother tongue instead of another language as a foreign language is to separate pupils and risk a school within a school. It also denies the bilingual student whose first language is not from Europe access to a European language other than English. In our experience the already bilingual student is more adept at learning a third or fourth language than the monolingual Anglophone.

Finally, I do not see it as always offering a lower status or less accessible possibility to have activities by choice after the final compulsory lesson. Indeed the opposite can be the case if properly handled.

5   Teaching through the mother tongue

The acceptance and relishing of bilingualism requires us to change the abhorrence of languages other than English and to allow them, indeed welcome them, into school. However, some fearing 'segregation' never like to 'withdraw' pupils according to their strongest language. The Swann report's Chapter 7 reveals a deep conflict between the Committee's wish to respect bilingualism but its abhorrence of 'withdrawal'. If there really is respect for a pupil's home language, why should there not be occasions when it is the main medium of a school activity?

The very word 'withdrawal' is a semantic trap as it has heavy connotations of the undesirable. Verity Khan has argued powerfully that the objection to all withdrawal is not compatible with a true intention to build up bilingualism (Khan, 1985). The report allows the possibility of teaching through the mother tongue in the early years - presumably because of the notion (not born out by the evidence) that only young bilingual children come into schools with very little English, and may need to have teachers use their strongest language for a while - but the sooner it is dropped by the school the better.

I should argue in precisely the opposite direction, and should wish to encourage teaching <u>through</u> the mother tongue. Little and Willey called for experiments in this in 1981 (Little and Willey, 1981, p.33), but there is still great resistance. There is some place for it throughout the years of education, but I should especially focus on two stages of language growth:

(a) The early stages of English:

Whilst the pupil has only very limited knowledge of the language of tuition she or he is being denied access to many aspects of the personality of the teacher and most of the tuition. Undoubtedly being in the English-taught class will help the pupil's English, but even with an E2L teacher present that growth will often be outweighed by the loss of growth in the subject. In these stages some teaching through the strongest language seems only fair - as indeed is a pupil's right in most states in the USA (c.f. Lau, 1974). Thus for some pupils I should wish, e.g., Humanities and Science to be taught in the pupil's strongest language for a period of time.

(b) Advanced Students:

As long ago as 1975 the Bullock report commented unhappily on a tendency to stop the specific teaching of English to bilingual students when they had reached a minimal stage. The Swann report would have us do the same for the mother tongue - 'maintain' it, but not 'teach' it. Yet growth in language requires the <u>use</u> of it in intellectually taxing contexts: unless you learn something through and in a language, unless you think, read, write, and struggle to extend your meaning in that language, it works only in the social and personal domain, and thus does not develop fully.

I should therefore wish to see some subjects in the fourth year secondary and above taught in a mother tongue - not because the pupil cannot learn the subject adequately in English, but because she or he will <u>extend</u> the mother tongue best that way.

Such options should be possible in large secondary schools, and Sixth Form Colleges, Tertiary Colleges, or FE Colleges. There are more practical difficulties over recruiting bilingual teachers than in any other aspect of my recommendations.

6   **Induction courses**

In some schools bilingual pupils arrive direct from other countries, speaking only a very little English, and with sometimes only the barest of basic vocabularies in English. Many of these pupils have come from schools very different from their new ones; some have had virtually no schooling. Everyone is agreed that these pupils should be integrated as soon as possible and have the fullest benefit from the new school. There is a question of how this is best achieved.

Observation and common sense suggest that rapid placement in and a sense of relationship within a pupil group is essential, but this alone will not give a promising move towards confidence in the new environment without some form of special induction course. Such a course is too glibly seen as 'separatist', when in fact it is likely to help towards a deeper and more real identification with the group and school than simply to let all concerned keep going with the normal routine - which offers so much that is baffling.

An induction or integration workshop or course would have a number of possible components, the balance between which would have to be established in each school for each pupil:

(a) Introduction in the strongest language to the whole family of the school, its people, its systems, and how to get the best out of it.

(b) Educational guidance to the pupil on the details of the school in her or his strongest language.

(c) Where necessary, a 'foundation' or 'introduction' to certain subjects, rather than only immediate entry into a class with no support in the strongest language.

(d) Mother-tongue teaching.

(e) E2L teaching in a group of about the same level to give a firm basis not possible in context.

(f) Special activities to help the new pupils to get to know other pupils - probably not best done in, e.g., standard curriculum subjects.

(g) Participation as appropriate in the start of timetabled subjects with which she or he will continue.

The mixture should not be the same as for a primary-secondary transfer of an English-speaking pupil - yet most schools manage a better induction for those pupils than the mid-term arrival of a pupil from a different educational tradition with very little English! The important ILEA study of movement into the secondary school (ILEA, 1985) has shown in detail the fears and needs of the regular transfer pupil - how much more is required by the bilingual, newly arrived, mid-year admission! - across the curriculum. For instance the approaches to Science teaching described in Teaching Language and Study Skills in Secondary Science (Bulman, 1984) can all be used. However we all need some specific training also.

7   The teaching of English

An appeal to a multilingual society and a consideration of the needs
of bilingual learners brings a new focus on language to all English
teaching in a school. For a school with bilingual learners there is
a greater willingness by pupils to be conscious about language.
Forms of English will be used by L2 speakers that are different from
those used by L1 speakers, and the differences can be explained.
Thus the unconscious usages that the L1 English speaker comes to
easily but which are so difficult to sense as an English L2 speaker
and are so difficult for L1 speakers to systematise and explain can
be fruitful ground for scrutiny - e.g. the phrasal verbs or the use
of the present perfect.

In a multilingual curriculum a conscious approach to the workings of
language will be essential, whether taught by 'English' teachers or
'languages' teachers for all pupils. Thus the 'foreign' languages
syllabuses and the 'English' syllabuses will complement each other.

It is now generally agreed that too much E2L teaching, whether in
separate centres or in schools, has been separated from other
aspects of the curriculum. Indeed there is a structural problem in
a school resulting from the division between departments of English,
Modern Languages, and E2L, sometimes with a little peripheral
'mother tongue'. A school needs to produce an overall policy for
bilingual learners which locates the E2L work in relationship to
bilingualism and the whole range of subjects.

This will certainly involve all teachers having some fairly sharp
understanding of how to teach E2L through the medium of their
subject and to help the bilingual learner understand the subject's
concepts and language. This is not different really from the
Bullock idea of 'language across the curriculum'. Exploring
concepts in technology such as 'permeable' and 'impermeable'
materials, to take a small example, must be a language lesson as
well as a concept lesson. All teachers need to be adept at
unpicking words to help all students see a way into them. (See
Marland 1977, p.p. 180-184 for a fuller discussion.) Techniques of
'subject teaching' developed for post-Bullock 'language across the
curriculum' work are adaptable for 'E2L'. The work is likely to
point up the need for a more conscious approach to the improvement
of skills in non-narrative reading (c.f. Marland, 1977 and 1978).
At the moment we largely stop teaching reading except in literature
once we have got people through the major phoneme / grapheme
relationships. A typical sentence from a typical book on canals
has: "It's surprising that although channels have been dug for
irrigation for centuries, very few people have ever thought of using
them for transport". That is not a bad sentence. But I've tried it
out on fourth-year classes, and more than half of mine don't know
what it means. They don't know whether they were used for transport

or weren't used for transport, because that kind of prose with connectives like 'if' and 'therefore' is not practised in fiction but only in non-fiction. Words like 'since' in fiction come up only in their temporal sense; in non-fiction they come up largely in their logical sense. You can do a full English course in many schools and have no practice in the reading of this kind of non-narrative prose. In a class I was teaching recently, most of the pupils didn't know the word 'prediction' in the sentence, "Do you consider these predictions could come true?" The question came after a list of predictions about the future in technology. Nobody had taught them that you don't really need to know what that word means because the word 'these' coming after a list must be pointing back to those things. So the reader can just leave 'predictions' as a blank: "Do you consider that these things that I've just told you about will come true?" Or the pupil could look at it the other way: they all know what a dictating machine is; they all know what a dictator is; they all know what 'pre-' means. They all ought to know that '-tion' is always an action. They only don't know it because we've stopped teaching the teaching of reading. If we were aware of language our pupils could work out the meaning of 'prediction' at that point.

An interesting test is the number of youngsters who know the word 'fantastic' but can't understand the word 'fantasy' when they meet it in a text. This is because no one has taught them to play around with parts of words. I should want a whole-school reading policy, for the most able, as well as the least able, that would have specific details in it and would ensure that all teachers are teachers of reading and vocabulary in their subject activity.

At other times there will be E2L specialists working alongside subject teachers - a partnership which requires far more working out than we have done so far. There will also, though, be times when a bilingual teacher is needed to explain the language of a subject fully and adequately.

Finally, contrary to the dominant view of Swann Chapter Seven, I am sure that some special E2L groups will be required at all levels. The equivalent of the apparently widely acceptable 'English for Special Needs' course at university, to support all bilingual undergraduates with the English needs of their courses, should be special English classes for most bilingual pupils within schools. Most of them need, respond to, and make good use of a more systematic and analytic approach to vocabulary, punctuation, and sentence structure than the monolingual anglophone finds valuable. The 'contextualised' learning of English 'in subjects' is essential, but it needs complementing with specific lessons in English devised for bilingual pupils.

8   Pastoral care

British schools are proud of their pastoral care, which is
'personal, educational, and vocational guidance'. This is language-
dependent, and requires a sensitive language interchange between
tutor and tutee. Almost by definition a monolingual tutor cannot
offer full pastoral care to a pupil whose strongest language is
other than the tutor's, unless the pupil's bilingual skills are very
fully developed. Bilingual pupils who currently have little English
are being denied their full pastoral care.

Very few schools have addressed themselves to this. The ILEA
working party of Division Two explored this challenge, and the
section on pastoral care is available in the second part of this
book. Their recommendation is one I should endorse: 'complementary
tutoring' is necessary in the tutee's strongest language, until her
or his English matches appropriately the tutoring needs or unless
her or his tutor speaks the tutee's strongest language adequately.

This is not to imply separation for many of the tutorial sessions,
but that a pattern of complementary tutoring should be integrated
with them.

9   Needs-based staffing

Obviously the education of bilingual learners requires additional
staffing which has to be based (as it is by State Law in most USA
states or by School Board regulations in Toronto, Canada) on the
language pattern of the school population. Clear formulae are
required for bilingual teachers and E2L teachers as part of a
coherent plan, and the staffing should be prospective, based on an
estimate of likely numbers, not retrospective on last year's
figures. Section II funding can, of course, be used.

This leads to the need for team leadership. Burnham points are
roll-based, but the scheme allows LEAs considerable flexibility, and
clearly this is going to be needed if the bilingual teams (including
E2L teachers) are to have adequate managerial strength without
taking from the other teams in a school.

I envisage regional/divisional bilingual centres to support the
teachers and to offer work with pupils in various languages where
the numbers are too low for schools to offer their own classes.

All questions of resourcing must be managed so that special-needs
staff for monolingual pupils are not removed. There is a danger of
unfairness both to monolingual black children and white ones if the
'special needs' pool is merely re-allocated for the needs of
bilingual learners and not increased appropriately.

Finally, there are the training implications of languages teachers. The dominance of French at University is possibly even increasing, and the enquiry by Sir James Gibbs on behalf of UCCA has shown that non-European languages are not only rarely taught but are courses under threat. Within university degree courses and certainly in PGCE and B.Ed. courses a greater range of linguistic diversity must be included, including specific introductions for all intending teachers to 'language awareness' courses and to non-European languages. The 'modern languages' teacher of today cannot be merely a French specialist. Some should be primarily specialists in Arabic, Gujerati, or other so far little-taught languages, and all must have a wide interest in and some knowledge of non-European languages.

10 Publishing

As part of the whole-school policy of language awareness and the encouragement of bilingualism it is essential to have in schools a range of books in and on languages other than English. We must find ways of stimulating more publishing in minority languages and of getting into schools the books and materials already published. For instance, I'd like to see a poetry anthology of translations into English of poems from a diversity of languages chosen for their suitability for and impact on pupils in English classrooms reading literature, but with each one facing its original version. I'd like to see more school library books for younger children that are bilingual (c.f. the excellent publications of the Middlesex Polytechnic edited by Jennie Ingham, (Ingham, 1984), and there is now a range available from a few ILEA support services).

CONCLUSION

Schools have to respond to the fact that the world is multilingual, much of our country is multilingual, and international communication is growing. Schools with bilingual pupils are lucky; they can build on the strength of those pupils' linguistic diversity and should offer a range of language experiences and languages to learn. Schools that have few if any bilingual pupils should have a very similar curriculum, preparing their pupils too for the richness of the multilingual world.

Bikhu Perekh has called the recent arrival of immigrants in our schools bringing a range of languages, many of them from outside Europe, a 'one-off bonus like North Sea oil (Perekh, 1986). It is an indictment of many of us that it took this 'bonus' to open our ears and our eyes to non-European languages. From this impact can come a thorough re-assessment of the place of languages in education, and a re-awakening of the curriculum to learn from and prepare for the multi-lingual world.

PART II

The education of bilingual learners

Towards a coherent policy

*Report of a working party on
bilingual education in Division Two
of the Inner London Education Authority*

CONTENTS

MEMBERS OF THE WORKING PARTY

Co-Chair:

Michael Marland   Head Teacher
North Westminster Community School

Laurie Goodhand   Head Teacher
Quinton Kynaston School
(until July, 1986)

Chris Adamson   Camden Committee for Community Relations

Diana Bailey   Head of English as a Second Language
North Westminster Community School
(until April, 1986)

Sue Barrow   Administrative Officer (Pupils)
DO2, ILEA

David Davies   Head of English as a Second Language
Quinton Kynaston School

Teresa Etim   Education Liaison Officer
Westminster Community Relations Council
(until October, 1986)

Fran Harmes   Borough Language Coordinator
Camden

Ali Haouas   Course Tutor
Centre for Urban Educational Studies

Davina Judelson   Community Worker - Team Leader
Community House Information Centre

Gwyn Robins   Divisional Education Officer
DO2, ILEA

Vi Tomlinson   Head Teacher
Gateway Primary School

Jim Wight   Inspector for Multi-Cultural Education
ILEA

1   INTRODUCTION: RACISM, BILINGUAL EDUCATION, AND THE NEED FOR A POLICY

1.1 The Conspiracy of Silence

To many people who speak only English, the ability to speak another language fluently is seen as a "problem", requiring sympathy. This is particularly true if that language is non-European. Although there is no firm evidence about attitudes of monolingual English-speaking people towards the different languages, it seems fair to say that people in general regard European languages, especially those of countries that have had long cultural ties with the United Kingdom, more favourably than non-European languages.

Indeed in British society there is a general cultural, political, artistic and social refusal to accept the reality of our linguistic richness. There is a virtual conspiracy of silence about what the Linguistic Minorities Project so aptly calls "the other languages of England":

> The overall national attitude towards linguistic diversity, and the patterns of social interaction which people experience in everyday life, affect language skills, and affect the relative value the different languages come to have for different members of the population, whether they can speak those languages or not. The implicit language policy of the national media, and of libraries with reference to the range of books stocked, as well as the choice of languages taught in schools and institutions of higher education, all have a bearing on the evolution of responses to the multilingualism of our society.   (Linguistic Minorities Project, 1985, p.9)

> The societal and the individual approaches to bilingualism are, of course, closely interrelated. If there is an unstated rule in many institutions such as offices, schools, restaurants or clubs that minority languages should not be used, at least with monolingual English speakers present, then the languages are likely to be limited to a very narrow range of functions. If, for example, programmes in minority languages on national radio or television channels are in practice restricted to unsocial hours, and if such languages are seldom if ever used in mainstream programmes, this too carries a message - though perhaps a different one for bilinguals and for monolinguals.   (ibid)

This resolutely monolingual facade of the public face of the country is further compounded by the presumption that there is a hierarchy of languages with French and German leading the field; Spanish way behind; and South Asian languages nearly ignored.

In the 1960s the multi-cultural debate started nationally with language, but it was largely an assimilation interpretation, with attention based almost solely on teaching English, and then only to the fairly early stages. The question of mother tongue was first widely discussed only in the 1970s, with the Bullock report in 1975 recommending:

> No child should be expected to cast off the language and culture of the home as he crosses the school threshold, and the curriculum should reflect those aspects of his life. (Committee of Enquiry, Rec. 249, p.543)

This statement would now be seen as important for all levels of education from nurseries and playgroups to further education.

The general effects of racism are still in the 1980s denied by many members of the dominant white culture, although many LEAs have made efforts to eradicate racism from all their work. However, the additional prejudices and difficulties which members of linguistic minorities have to suffer have been less thoroughly documented and less strenuously fought. In education, policies to fight this double prejudice and to enable all to benefit from bilingualism have not been developed either by central government or even by local authorities.

Until recently, there has only been patchy and marginal teaching of other languages as mother tongue. As the Centre for Information on Language Teaching and Research observed as long ago as 1976, there are "in Britain and particularly in England ... many thousands of bilingual children whose mother tongues are largely ignored educationally" (CILT, 1975, p.7). Indeed the majority of the teaching profession and many members of the public still bring their English-centric attitudes to bear, and further argue that retaining and developing the mother tongue confuses the pupil and impedes the learning of English. The EEC Directive of 1977 (EEC, 1977; and c.f. the commentary in Commission for Racial Equality, 1980) has hardly impinged, and the DES circular to implement it was not issued until July 31, 1981 (DES 1981), six days after all Member States should have complied! Unlike, for instance, Belgium, Bavaria, France, or Denmark, the UK has not followed this Directive by establishing the numbers of pupils concerned (Commission of the European Communities, 1984, p. UK. 1) and the DES states that "it is impossible to give a comprehensive summary of the measures taken to receive pupils whose mother tongue is not English" (op. cit., p. UK. 2)! No wonder that the comments by the Commission are tart, especially criticising the fact that: "Even according to the most favourable estimates integrated tuition in the language and culture of origin is offered to only 2.2% of pupils whose first language is not English" (op. cit., p. UK. 6).

An important Schools Council Study, Multi-Ethnic Education: The Way Forward, completed and published in 1981, criticised the lack of progress over the previous ten years. It drew up a large number of recommendations, saying:

> If the findings of the survey are accepted and if the objectives of the 1977 Green Paper that 'the curriculum should reflect a sympathetic understanding of the different cultures and races that now make up our society' is to be released ... action is necessary.
> (Little and Willey, 1981, pp.32-34)

There is very little evidence that this recommendation has been seriously followed up, although the Schools Council did initiate an important project, now continued by the Schools Curriculum Development Committee. Encouragingly there are a number of small projects, including the bilingual story publishing by the Middlesex Polytechnic, led by Jennie Ingham, the ILEA's "Community Languages Resources Scheme", and the Punjabi Language Development Board in Birmingham. Two valuable journals cover aspects of the field: The Bilingual Family Newsletter and Multicultural Teaching. Some evidence of "a growing network of support for bilingualism" is found by the SCDC project (Tansley and Craft, 1984, p.367), which senses after its three-year study "increasing efforts of LEAs to meet the needs of such children" (ibid., p.382). About one third of LEAs now have a policy on mother-tongue teaching, but there appears to be no evidence from the survey that even those who have developed some form of mother-tongue-teaching policy have related this to the other components (especially teaching through the mother tongue) that must make up a true bilingual education policy.

The ILEA took an important step in endorsing the teaching of mother tongue in Report 2321, an important and far-seeing policy document, which recommended "an inspector for mother-tongue teaching to be appointed to work as part of the modern languages inspectorate" (ILEA, 1982, p.7), an appointment fulfilled in 1984 that has already led to important improvements. However, that policy document was only a beginning, and importantly it was unable:

(a) to produce formulae for mother-tongue staffing;

(b) to consider the key issue of some "subject" or "content" teaching at certain stages being in the pupil's mother tongue;

(c) to produce a coherent overall bilingual education policy.

Although he had a genuine regard for the learning of languages, and

34

has pointed out that "The acquistion of linguistic skills is a rich and fascinating field for study" (Joseph, 1984, p.3), the former Secretary of State, Sir Keith Joseph, was really quite discouraging, as if he considered that linguistic minority communities needed protecting from the ambitions of the education system to force unwanted tuition onto families, and as if the fact that there were logistical difficulties in teaching all languages should prevent the teaching of those where it was possible. He declared that "it is not feasible for state schools to offer mother-tongue tuition to each pupil as of right", arguing both on the grounds of practicality ("We have neither the suitably qualified teachers to cover such numbers nor the financial resources to support them") and on the grounds of "the desirable limits of state intervention", stressing that "where the family's free choice is to maintain the language, then it is for relatives and friends and the wider community to explore the achievement of that end through voluntary and non-publicly provided funds" (ibid, p.1). Despite his welcome encouragement of the creation in state schools of a "background atmosphere within the school which encourages children to respect other cultures and to admire proficiency in more than one language" (ibid. p.2) and his admirable stressing that "linguistic minorities need not be seen as having a problem - lack of practice in English - but as having an asset, a skill in language" (ibid. p.2), this Secretary of State gave very little encouragement towards the development of mother tongues and the education of bilingual learners.

The lack of a national policy to which an LEA can refer has been bitterly commented on by others. In 1981 a consultation at the Commission for Racial Equality drafted a resolution that spoke for many:

> This Conference feels extremely concerned that the DES and ILEA are only paying token or no notice to the EEC directives to teach parental languages of the minority communities. In the face of enormous institutional and other forms of racism prevalent in Britain, the CRE, in co-operation with the local communities' efforts, should begin to campaign for the total acceptance and recognition of these languages as second languages which must be taught in the mainstream education system. The campaign also demands adequate resources for developing curriculum teaching materials; and the training of teachers and other teachers who are already employed by the LEA's.
>
> (CRE, 1981, p.9)

It is regrettable that this complaint had still to be made three years later. Reporting a conference in April 1984 of mother-tongue teachers of Punjabi, the Times Educational Supplement wrote:

Conference members also critized the Department of Education and Science for having no policy on mother-tongue teaching even though Britain had ostensibly accepted the EEC directive.

(Times Educational Supplement, 12.8.84)

The following month the ILEA published the report of the Committee chaired by Dr Hargreaves. This report encouragingly devoted considerable space to "pupils for whom English is a second language and bilingual or multilingual pupils" (Committee on the Curriculum and Organisation of Secondary Schools, 1984, pp. 45-48). However, bilingual education was not the brief of the Committee, and it too found itself referring primarily to the English as a Second Language (E2L) aspect, with only a tantalisingly brief glimpse of bilingual education when it recommends in "group work and inquiry-based learning" that "children should be encouraged to pursue this in part in their mother tongue"; it also suggests that "advice should be sought from the appropriate inspectors and advisory teachers about ways of providing supplementary mother-tongue resources within mainstream classes" (op. cit., p.49). Valuable as the attitude of the report is, the fragments still do not offer a coherent approach to the education of bilingual learners.

More recently still, HMI have published an informal survey of mother-tongue teaching in a handful of Local Education Authorities (HMI, 1984). It is obviously pleasing that there is now some HMI coverage of the mother-tongue element of bilingual education, but it has to be noted that their findings were fairly depressing, and it was disappointing that no clear recommendations were made.

One especially acute result of the lack of policy as compared with Canada, USA, and Sweden, or, near to home, Wales, is the inability to produce the resources for bilingual education, especially the teachers of E2L and mother-tongue teachers required. Heads and inspectors are constantly negotiating and persuading long after the children are in the school and require teaching. This failure of resources to keep up with the pressure for places in schools has even led to the scandalous position of bilingual pupils being out of school for weeks and months, or in school but receiving no tuition in E2L or their mother tongue and unable to comprehend English-medium teaching.

In this depressing overall situation it is inevitable that the institutional racism which oppresses all black people will affect bilingual learners in an additional number of specific ways, and may lead to pupils failing to reach their full potential to be able to take their appropriate place in society:

(a) Failure by the school to give recognition to the mother tongue (even sometimes open hostility to it when used in school) devalues a child's home and cultural experience in his or her own eyes.

(b) The beginner in English who may have one or two special classes but spends the rest of her or his time at the back of the class understanding little or nothing is being denied access to the curriculum and learning.

(c) Even the third-stage learner can have difficulty in understanding more complex concepts unless language support is provided. There may also be literacy difficulties when written fluency in the English language may consciously or unconsciously be a part of the assessment. (See Broadbent et al., 1983)

(d) Conversely, too much time spent in specialised E2L lessons away from the normal class may have the effect of denying access to learning which is being given to the peer group.

(e) Failure to consult the child and her or his parents as to the way in which provision is made can all too easily be seen as cultural arrogance in a school structure where power is nearly always in the hands of white, English-speaking people.

Even where strenuous efforts have been made by members of minority communities, parents, teachers, administrators, and pupils, the provision is essentially patchy, adding a teacher here or a class there. <u>Above all the education system has not developed a philosophy of bilingual education.</u> Too often the "multi-cultural" debate stops short of language. Teachers treat "E2L children" almost as if they are a transitory "problem" that will go away, rather than realising that:

a) bilingualism is a permanent and important aspect of British and world life (e.g. some 56,000 ILEA school children are bilingual, as is 70% of the world population);

b) bilingualism is a strength in the individual and a gain for society;

c) modern evidence shows considerable cognitive advantages from the development of bilingual skills (e.g. Cummins, 1983);

d) the presence of bilingual pupils can and should be a gain for initially monolingual pupils;

e) the challenge of bilingualism cannot be met by merely adding a few E2L teachers to the timetable, and a few mother-tongue teachers to out-of-hours classes.

There is no well investigated study of the education of bilingual learners as there has been, for instance, of the teaching of mathematics or science. The most careful official national statement is the brief eleven-page chapter in the Bullock report (Committee of Enquiry, 1975, pp.284-94), and it firmly concluded:

> There should be further research into the teaching of their own language to children of immigrant communities and into the various aspects of bilingualism in schools.
>   (ibid, sec. 266. p.545)

The Director of CILT stressed that 'the performances of such children (i.e. those "pupils who themselves had to learn English as a second language") in a second language would well repay detailed study' (CILT, 1976, p.12). The Linguistic Minorities Project has provided some research into the range and extent of languages other than English, but its conclusions are depressing:

> Many of the ethnic minority community languages in England are at present ignored or devalued as an individual and societal resource, when in fact their speakers could with minimal investment have their existing skills developed during their school years, and thus offer the country an educational, economic and political resource of considerable value. And the value of minority languages lies not only in what they offer to the large number of bilingual members of our society. Bilingualism in our society also offers the possibility of changing the narrowly monolingual perspective of many majority institutions and individuals.   (op. cit., pp.162-163)

The Project recommends that policies should be developed. However, no detailed help is available from the DES. Despite the seventeen items of research listed in a CILT publication (CILT, 1976, pp 94-96), those responsible for curriculum planning in schools have few results of relevant research to ponder and use for their curriculum development.

The UK approach so far has been to struggle for resources, adding E2L and Mother Tongue separately to a system otherwise hardly affected by bilingualism. This contrasts sharply with the more coherent approaches in many continental European countries, Australia, Canada, and the USA.

Both Sweden's Directive 1981:49 and the USA's Bilingual Act of 1970 guarantee heritage language teaching as of right. There is also a firm legislative and policy background in other countries: Canada, for instance, has had legislation since 1980, and a Minister of State for Multiculturalism. Sweden has had legislation since 1968, with frequent later improvements. For instance, since an Ordinance of 21 June, 1979, children who are still monolingual in a language have a legal right to be taught their home language and be given other lessons in that language. Swedish is then successively introduced as the teaching language. In the USA, federal legislation has established the right of "heritage language teaching" and, indeed, a full bilingual education. The historic 1974 USA Federal Government Court ruling led to the essential needs of bilingual pupils being embodied in legislation. The Court ruled importantly:

> There is no equality of treatment by providing students with the same facilities, teachers and curriculum. For students who do not understand English are effectively foreclosed from a meaningful education. (Lau, 1974)

This simple but fundamental truth was expressed in legislation and then in mandatory policies. (Some other examples of ruling and policy are given in Appendix B.) School districts and schools as a result have been able to develop coherent educational policies for bilingual pupils, which consider the pupils' overall educational experience, as well as their right to and need for mother-tongue development and when appropriate for teaching through the pupil's mother tongue. From clearly articulated aims and policies have come coherent bilingual education practices and mandatory resourcing.

1.2 **A Policy for Equality**

Over a period of perhaps twenty years the attitude of enlightened LEAs has moved from a perspective emphasising mainly assimilation through one concentrated on cultural diversity to the present policy primarily emphasising equality. A parallel development has taken place in the education of bilingual pupils. Initially pupils who did not speak English were sent to special centres for the teaching of E2L. Pupils were then expected to be assimilated into the culture of the majority and there was therefore virtually no concern for the maintenance of the community language. Later there was more emphasis on pupils being taught English at school, but there was still little regard for the maintenance of their own language, still less its development.

A third phase has now developed. Sometimes called cultural pluralism, this phase accepts the rights of pupils to be educated in and through their own tongue. It also recognises Creole as a language in its own right. A multi-ethnic policy is indeed meaningless unless it includes positive attitudes to bilingualism and adequate resources for educating bilingual learners. A policy for equality involves a bilingual education policy.

As the leader of the ILEA, Francis Morrell, spelt out, the centrality of mother-tongue development within the multi-ethnic curriculum must be recognised:

> Some groups of black children have specific needs - for example those who speak English as their second language. Rightly our schools make a tremendous effort to ensure that these children acquire the skills of reading, writing, and speaking English. However, we believe that literacy means being able to read and write in one's own language. Children who can read and write in their own language are better able to cope with a second language, and even a third. It is our policy therefore, over a period, to provide facilities for this teaching within our schools for our bilingual children, who are not a problem but an asset to our schools and communities.
>
> (ILEA, 1983, p.6)

To strengthen such commitment a coherent bilingual education policy is required, which will consider and inter-relate all aspects of education for bilingual pupils and their peers. Such a policy needs to:

(a) relate the pupils' process of learning across the curriculum at all levels of education to their mother-tongue development and their acquisition of English;

(b) establish the most appropriate contexts for mother-tongue development and for significant uses of the mother tongue in intellectual and study growth;

(c) recognise that bilingualism is not merely a language issue, and the effect of failing to develop bilingual education in schools is to perpetuate a form of institutional racism;

(d) devise ways of helping the education of all pupils to be enriched by their bilingual peers and the bilingual curriculum;

(e) provide a focus for the views and wishes of minority-language communities with whom we work, and incorporate ways of consulting with and being accountable to them;

(f) relate resourcing to curriculum needs;

(g) encourage further investigation, consultation, and research to help develop better provision of bilingual education.

2   A PHILOSOPHY OF BILINGUAL EDUCATION

2.1   Introduction

In this discussion the term "bilingual" is used to describe any
child who regularly uses two languages.   It does not necessarily
signify full command of both.   For many years these children have
been the focus of educational attention if their English is
considered inadequate for them to participate fully in mainstream
classroom activities.   Bilingual children have not been seen in
positive terms, but negatively, on a scale of their competence in
English.   It is the intention of this paper to propose that
educational provision should be oriented not just towards pupils'
English learning needs, but also to their needs and potential as
bilingual learners.   We are seeking for a coherent overall
philosophy of bilingual education which will inform our practical
planning.   (Part of the argument that follows has been developed
from the ILEA committee document   Bilingualism in the ILEA -The
Educational Implications of the 1981 Language Census, ILEA, 1982.)

2.2   The role of language in learning

The starting point for constructing a sound policy towards the
education of bilingual learners must be neither the importance of
English nor the significance of the mother tongue but the role of
language itself in the educational development of the children, and
the recognition that there are many families where a language other
than English is, and will remain, the predominant language.
Language is critical in fundamental educational processes like
concept-acquistion and inquiry, the understanding of cause and
effect, and interpreting and evaluating evidence.   The ability to do
these things is developed in and through all languages.   The Bullock
Report, A Language for Life, made a central statement about the role
of language in learning in UK schools.

> Their bilingualism is of great importance to the children
> and their families, and also to society as a whole.   In a
> linguistically conscious nation in the modern world we
> should see it as an asset, as something to be nurtured,
> and one of the agencies that should nurture it is the
> school.   Certainly the school should adopt a positive
> attitude towards its pupils' bilingualism and wherever
> possible should help maintain and deepen their knowledge
> of their mother tongues.
> (Committee of Enquiry, 1975, p.294)

The report saw the recognition and fostering of mother tongue as
complementing rather than hindering the learning of English as a
second language.

Confidence and ability in this language (i.e. the mother
tongue) will help the children to the same qualities in
their second language, English.   (ibid.)

2.3 Access to English

In schools and in linguistic minority communities it is
unambiguously recognised that the pupils' control of English must be
developed as rapidly as possible from whatever level they have
reached on entry to school. This is very important both in order to
obtain access to the curriculum in school and in order to equip
pupils fully for life and work outside school. For several decades,
many LEAs have been developing and extending provision for the
teaching of English as a second language. There is much evidence of
skilled, dedicated, and successful practice in this, and an evolving
pattern of school response in which all teachers in multilingual
schools, and not just E2L teachers, are involved. But there are
also clear indications that this provision needs to be improved and
strengthened if the objective of equipping all bilingual children
fully for life and work is to be achieved. This is so both in the
early stages, when resources are not being deployed rapidly enough,
and in later stages. The Bullock Committee put this forcefully many
years ago:

> The situation can be summed up as one in which the
> teaching often starts too late and ends too soon.
>   (Committee of Enquiry, 1975, p.289)

The Committee made a sustained plea for the continuation of the
teaching of English to advanced standards:

> We regard it as a grave disservice to such children to
> deprive them of sustained English teaching after they have
> been learning English for only a comparatively short time
> ... But there is little evidence in the schools and
> centres we visited of really advanced English language
> work of this nature.   (op. cit., pp.290 - 291)

Sadly, nearly a decade later, in the ILEA, the Hargreaves Committee
expressed similar criticisms:

> We also feel anxiety about pupils who become fluent in the
> language of the playground, and who express themselves
> with reasonable clarity on paper, since these are commonly
> assumed to have made themselves equal educationally with
> their indigenous peers and are usually not given further
> support. Experience has shown that this assumption is
> ill-founded. Such children may find themselves
> inadequately rooted in two languages, since a restrictive

form of English may have partially ousted their original mother tongue from their homes, and when their studies reach the more sophisticated levels of many post-16 courses, they lack the verbal competence to express abstract concepts or arguments in both their languages.
(Committee on the Curriculum and Organisation of Secondary Schools, 1984, para. 3.7.6., p.46)

2.4 Promoting and developing the 'mother tongue'

The second, complementary, strand in a philosophy of bilingual education concerns the promotion and development of mother tongues. 'Mother tongue' is in many ways an unsatisfactory term. For this reason other terms like 'community language', 'heritage language', and 'home language' are often used. In this discussion the terms 'mother tongue' or 'community language' are used to describe the first language spoken by the pupil's family or the national language of which it is a variant or close relative. In a small minority of cases, it may not literally be the strongest language of the child's home. For instance, many children with Bangladeshi parents speak Sylheti, which though related to Bengali is also different from it in a number of significant ways. But literacy in standard Bengali is the target of the community-run classes attended by thousands of Sylheti-speaking children. Similarly, children from Punjabi-speaking Moslem families will seek to become literate in the closely-related national language of Urdu.

2.5 Eight reasons for developing pupils' mother tongues

(a) Education is concerned with developing the abilities and potential of all children. Any child's mother tongue, be it English or another language, is a strength produced by years of continuous learning, with enormous potential for further development.

(b) The bilingual child's mother tongue is an important potential channel for his or her learning, and at certain times and for certain aspects of the curriculum will be the best medium for it.

(c) The education system has long attempted to meet the objective of bilingualism for English-speaking children, through the teaching of French, German, and other European languages. The rationale for promoting this sort of "bilingualism" is a strong one. There are <u>intellectual</u> advantages for the pupil who is enabled to see that there are other ways of conceptualising and interpreting the world around us and to develop a greater awareness of the relationship between the language people use

43

and the objects and ideas to which the language refers. There are cultural advantages because of the more direct access that pupils can gain to the literature and the cultural systems of other societies. There are the functional advantages of being able to use the second language in a variety of situations, commercial and social. All these arguments that exist for English-speaking children who learn other languages apply, often with greater force, in the case of already bilingual children whose first language is other than English.

(d) The mother tongue is an important part of a pupil's cultural or ethnic identity. If it is valued and encouraged in school, it is very likely to enhance the child's self-image and confidence, and to influence the child's status with his or her peers.

(e) Bilingual children need to maintain their language if they are not to cut themselves off linguistically from their families and communities. There has been a regrettable tendency among educationists to consider children's bilingualism as a transitional phenomenon and that children should inevitably move from using a home language out of necessity to using English out of preference. It is important to remember that the bilingual child's main medium of communication in the home and in the home community (including the country from which the family may have come to England, however long ago) will in all likelihood remain the child's first language. Educational institutions are surely bound to provide that child with the opportunities to develop his or her own potential within that community as well as within the wider community where English is the dominant language.

(f) The vigorous inclusion of teaching of and through the mother tongue is a critical way of showing both the minority communities and others that Britain does indeed recognise cultures and languages other than English and wishes to maintain them within a developing British culture.

(g) Britain as a multi-ethnic society needs proficient bilinguals who can not only meet the interpreting, translating, and liaising needs that exist within our society and between Britain and other parts of an increasingly interdependent world, but can also fulfil executive and administrative roles in commercial and public organisations more effectively because of their bilingualism.

(h) Being fully proficient and literate in both mother tongue and English extends the career and life-options for the bilingual child.

2.6 Are languages in competition in learning?

Some people, both amongst teachers and outside schools, are worried about the effects of teaching pupils two or more languages: Will the promotion of pupils' mother tongues result in their learning English less well? Since so many people in the world live in bilingual or multilingual communities (probably some seventy percent), and many education systems involve some sort of bilingual policy, it is possible to look at two sorts of evidence. The first is about the effect of being bilingual on the educational developments of pupils. The second is about the effect of different sorts of educational provision that seek to teach the mother tongues of linguistic minority pupils or to use them as a medium of instruction.

Early studies into the effect of bilingualism on educational and intellectual development tended to conclude that bilingualism was a handicap. But research over the last two decades has increasingly challenged the validity of the earlier findings and produced evidence that, if all the other factors that influence educational performance and intellectual development are taken into account (which the earlier studies regularly failed to do), bilingualism is no disadvantage, and may in some respects be a distinct advantage. The largest, most recent study in the UK which bears on this issue is the 1984 Assessment of Performance Unit report on the reading and writing performance of pupils in secondary schools (Gorman et al., 1982). In the Welsh part of the survey, they found no significant difference in performance in English between the majority who were monolingual English speakers and the substantial minority who were Welsh/English bilinguals. Across the world it is now widely accepted in the academic community that bilingual education not only does not hinder language acquisition in the second language, but assists it. Indeed some studies have appeared to show a definite cognitive gain (e.g. Cummins, 1983). It appears that the former Secretary of State for Education, Sir Keith Joseph, accepted that research evidence supports the use of the mother tongue teaching at least in the early stages of education, and his declaration at the EEC Mother Tongue Coloquium in March, 1984, can be taken as the official acceptance of the research:

> Some while ago there was a belief that the move to English should be abrupt, and that any continued use of mother tongue would interfere with that process. The latest evidence is that this is not the case - that the child's cognitive development can be enhanced by some use of the mother tongue in class at the primary stage.
>
> (Joseph, 1984, p.2)

Sweden summed up its attitude in legislation ten years ago in a strong statement on the intellectual value of bilingual education:

Recent research into language learning, linguistic development, and bilingualism has shown that a child, denied the opportunity of developing its mother tongue to an abstract level and confronted in school with instruction in another language, is subjected to heavy intellectual and emotional strain. This can seriously disrupt a child's development. On the other hand, children making a complete change of language at an early age may encounter serious problems of parental contact. What is more, the acquisition of a second language is greatly facilitated by the child having a knowledge of its own mother tongue. The Commission, therefore, maintains that society should safeguard the right of the child to its mother tongue. Greater efforts should be made within the school system to offer all children the opportunity of developing their mother tongue.

(Commission on Migrants' Languages
and Culture, 1984, p.12)

It is not easy to generalise directly from studies about different sorts of bilingual educational provision. This is mainly because most of the studies are concerned with different forms of bilingual education in which pupils receive a substantial part of their general education through their mother tongue. A "substantial part" means anything from half-time (as in the Bradford/EEC Project) to full-time (as in some Welsh-medium schools). This type of bilingual education is also often focussed on the early years of a child's education and designed as a bridge between home, where one language is spoken, and the school system which uses another language. However, there is substantial experience of various mixtures in, for instance, Massachusetts with Puerto Rican pupils in Spanish/English bilingual programmes and Canada with French/English bilingual programmes. One review stated that a study of the relevant research "would be likely to lead an enquirer to the conclusion that there is no a priori reason to assume that the educational use of pupils' first language will impair the learning of standard English in the course of an efficiently organised educational programme; nor does the experimental evidence support such an assumption" (Gorman, 1982, p.p. 4 and 5).

Indeed, in schools where literacy in English is both a goal and a tool from the outset, those pupils who are not literate in their first or home language may be doubly handicapped if they are not given the chance to develop literacy skills in that language. Literacy is essentially a matter of associating symbols alone or in groups with sounds and meanings. Bilingual pupils who have not begun to get to grips with this process in their first language will understandably have commensurably greater difficulty in developing those skills in what is, and will probably remain, their second (or third) language. The greater the skill in the first language, the greater the ease of developing a high level of skills in other languages.

2.7 Teaching and using pupils' mother tongues: five principles

There are five strong basic principles for developing pupils' mother tongues:

(a) It is the right of all bilingual children to know that their mother-tongue skills are recognised and valued in schools. This goes beyond the gesture, worthwhile beginning though it is, of placing a few multilingual signs around the buildings. That is recognition but fails to demonstrate that a child's language is valued. This can come only from according community languages appropriate status within a multi-ethnic and anti-racist curriculum. It entails, at the least, providing children with real opportunities to develop and use their lingusitic skills in the classroom, and providing adequate translator/interpreter services where the need exists.

(b) It is educationally desirable that bilingual children in primary schools should be given the chance to extend their oral skills and to read and write their mother tongues. This implies that the mother tongues will not only be taught as subjects in their own right but used functionally when appropriate as a means of instruction and development in other curriculum areas. As the mother tongues are living languages, pupils should have the opportunity at all stages of improving their oral proficiency. They should be used freely within the schools as a normal medium of communication and expression and should be integrated across the curriculum.

(c) It is educationally desirable that bilingual children in secondary schools should be given the chance to study the language and literature of their home as a subject on the school curriculum and to gain appropriate examination qualifications.

(d) The mother-tongue skills of bilingual children are a valuable potential channel for supporting their learning, and in a number of circumstances as the medium in which teaching should take place.

(e) All children should have the opportunity to learn how other languages work and be encouraged to take an interest in and be informed about the languages spoken by their peers and neighbours.
An understanding of a second language is already considered an essential part of the general curriculum. The "World

Languages" Programme" or "Language Awareness" courses now being used in a number of schools offer the opportunity for community languages to be used, discussed, and taught in the classroom. There is a need for further initiatives along these lines, which will also include the aim of giving status to community languages, and so, indirectly, to the children who speak those languages. Thus the teaching of mother tongues increases the range of languages in the school, and considerably heightens the intensity of the language climate for all.

2.8 Conclusion

We reject the categorisation of pupils by their control of English, and we also seek to eradicate the fear of other languages. We see as a natural right and a logical interpretation of the 1944 Education Act that children whose first language is not English have a full right to teaching of and in English, to development of their mother tongue, and to teaching through the medium of their mother tongue. Our philosophy of bilingual education "celebrates and encourages the total range of the pupil's linguistic competencies" (the Hargreaves' Committee's phrase, 3.7.8., p.46) and recognises the range of languages in a school as a strength for all. When pupils are young they should have a combination of modes of tuition, and when they are older they should be able to move easily and by their choice between lessons and activities in more than one language.

Those schools with a number of bilingual pupils who bring as first languages those other than English have an immense advantage in some of the central educational aims, a point which is forcefully put by the Swedish Commission:

> Not even persons remaining in their countries of origin for their whole lives will in future be able to isolate themselves and avoid contact with foreign languages and cultures. All children, in both immigration and emigration countries, will need to learn that they form part of a wider community outside their own village, city and country. We will all have to learn to associate with people across national boundaries.
>
> (Commission on Migrants' Languages and Culture, 1984, p.3)

How lucky, therefore, are pupils whose education can be helped by the presence of bilingual pupils.

3   KEEPING IN TOUCH WITH THE COMMUNITIES WE SERVE

3.1 Communication with parents

Over the last twenty years there has been intermittent encouragement
for improving home-school links from Newsom (Central Advisory
Council for Education, 1963, para. 204 and recommendation (d),
pp.70-71), through Plowden (Central Advisory Committee, 1967, pp.37-
49) and Bullock (Committee of Inquiry, 1975, pp.519-520), to Rampton
(Committee of Inquiry, 1981, pp.79-80). Yet thorough field research
published by the EEC shows how far the UK is behind most EEC
countries in many aspects of home/school links (Macbeth, 1984).

There is a need for both LEAs and schools to develop policies on
home-school liaison which specifically focus on the interests of
bilingual families. For instance, the ILEA document
Race, Sex and Class 3: A Policy for Equality: Race recommends the
removal of "those practices and procedures which discriminate
against black pupils/students and their families" (ILEA, 1983 (c)
iv p.6), and argues the need for "developing new kinds of
consultation", in which minority groups have "considerably more
power and opportunity than hitherto to express and communicate their
views and to participate in decisions which affect everyone ....."
(ibid, (c) ii p.6).

In developing arrangements for teaching mother tongue and in other
ways promoting bilingualism, schools should consult with the parents
concerned and seek to co-operate with mother-tongue classes
organised by the community groups and other agencies. Ways must be
found to work in partnership to support and encourage the excellent
work already being done.

3.2 The flow of information

The community of a school consists of several groups in addition to
pupils, staff, and governors. It is with these other groups that we
are concerned here - the families of pupils, community
organisations, mother-tongue classes for all ages, and residents and
workers in the geographical area of the school. Basic to the
relationship between a school and its wider communities is the
information process both to and from the school. At present, many
schools make genuine efforts to communicate information to parents
through widespread use of newletters, parents' associations,
information evenings, report evenings, and open days. However, as
these are with rare exceptions conducted purely in English there are
many parents and community organisations excluded from this process
including those who are unable to read.

There is clearly a need for a flexible and adaptable pool of translators and interpreters (the two are not the same) to facilitate the process. Communications must be in the strongest language of families. This not only eases communication; it indicates respect for the language and culture of the families, and goes some way towards putting people at ease and allowing a genuine dialogue to take place.

Most schools have arrangements whereby newsletters, bulletins, invitations, and the like are distributed periodically. Few schools have either the time or the resources to ensure that these communications are in a form which can be understood by people who speak or read in a language other than English. Consequently, significant sections of the school community do not take part in this information process. There is, therefore, a need for paid translation services to be made available to schools on a flexible needs basis in order that at least major communications from the school can be transmitted in a form intelligible to those language groups which comprise a significant part of the school's community. One suggested model for this service is that where speakers of a language exceed a certain number (perhaps ten) then access to translation services for that language should be mandatory for a school; where speakers of a language exceed a larger number, or some specified proportion of a school's enrolment, then that school should have permanent access to some form of area translation service. If this kind of provision is not made then it cannot be claimed that all students and their families have equality of access to the school.

The initial interview, when a family seeks admission for a pupil to the school, is for English-speaking families an exchange of views and information about the student, about schooling, and about the school in particular. The student's background, education, interests, and abilities form one side of this exchange, and information on the local education system, the organisation of the school, its rules, its ethos, and its practices form the bulk of the other. Few schools are able to have these interviews conducted in any language other than English, and even when a bilingual relative or friend accompanies the student with families whose strongest language is other than English misunderstandings are frequent and misinformation is passed. A common situation for the non-English speaking applicant is that a place is vacant, an offer is made and a starting date fixed, yet student and interviewer know nothing about each other. The initial interview is an occasion when as a matter of course interpreters should be available where necessary in order to ensure that an interview worthwhile for pupil, family, and school does take place.

A third major aspect of the home-school information process which often discriminates against the families of bilingual pupils is the arrangements for parents' evenings. Low attendance at events of this kind by parents of linguistic minority pupils is sometimes erroneously interpreted as a sign of apathy or of poor family support for their children's education. Schools need to examine their own practices and procedures in order to make them accessible to these families. Reasons have been found on investigation to be primarily practical rather than indications of apathy: unsocial working hours, language difficulties, transport difficulties, unwillingness to go out at night, and the fact that the school is often the only major English institution with which parents have to relate are predominant among these. Schools could investigate the possibility of establishing more flexible ways of involving linguistic minority parents in these occasions, for example by using translation/interpretation services as a matter of course for parents' evenings, by experimenting with day-time sessions, and by using bilingual students as 'greeters' and 'guides'. When appropriate, special meetings could be held.

Often the bilingual child in a family in which parents speak little or no English plays a major interpreting and translating role. These children are often used by their parents to communicate with schools, shops, hospitals, housing offices, and the DHSS in the home area. These pupils often bring to school considerable practical skills as bilingual workers within the family. This has two separate but complementary implications:

(a) Such pupils could both extend their skills and help the school if they were to be involved in a variety of tasks and consultation. These pupils must, however, not be exploited by the school.

(b) The school will have to help familiarise these pupils with the basic knowledge to carry out this function. One teacher has said: "I am consulted three or four times a week by Bangladeshi pupils on matters such as housing, rights, benefits, and ways of using existing channels."

The flow of information between schools and the communities they serve must be a two-way process. Schools must communicate to families information about the education system, about the curriculum, about rules and structures of the school, and about parental rights. Parents have a right to this information, which is at present not available to large numbers of families by virtue of the fact that their language is not English. Parents also have a right to raise their own questions at schools, the right to seek and bring information, make requests and proposals, and seek changes. At present for the most part these rights are restricted to articulate English-speaking families. Here we are concerned that they be extended to those families whose home language is a language other than English.

3.3 Outreach strategies

The communication gap between schools and bilingual communities has
many causes, but the central cause is the lack of shared culture and
language. This suggests three things:

(a) LEAs appoint or fund people who can go out and take the
     discussion into the community, into people's homes - who can
     help playgroups, nurseries, and the school to connect with the
     community and vice versa.

(b) These people should speak the language and share the culture of
     the communities with whom they are liaising.

(c) There is a need for educational advice and support to bilingual
     communities which, whilst maintaining a close relationship with
     the educational system (and being funded by it) is provided by
     an independent agency.

Contact between school and those communities represented within the
school should provide an opportunity for all children to explore
their own cultural heritage. Consultation with the local community
is vital. The following would be appropriate:

(a) use of school by community groups;

(b) recognition of particular cultural activities, e.g. religious
     festivals, public holidays, and the right to dress in
     accordance with tradition;

(c) need for all communities to represent their views to the school
     at all meetings, Governing Body, School Councils, etc;

(d) distribution of information;

(e) access to educational advice from independent sources;

(f) right to negotiate and determine education choices and
     priorities.

There are many strategies that can be followed for schools and a
local education authority to achieve these goals:

(a) The more staff, teaching and non-teaching, that schools, pre-
     school groups, and other educational agencies employ who speak
     the languages and share the culture of the bilingual
     communities, the more the normal school and pre-school
     procedures for communicating with parents will be successful.
     This is not a question of positive discrimination towards the
     bilingual teachers but of appointing staff who meet the
     linguistic needs of an area.

Since in many situations where bilingual parents are in communication or negotiation with schools the power relationship is heavily weighted against the parents and it is easy for them to be inhibited about expressing what they really feel and want, partly because of status and partly knowledge, community liaison people of the sort described in (b) and (c) can play an important advisory role giving both knowledge and support to the parents involved.

(b) A school should build up its knowledge of people currently working in the communities whose role is to provide information and a liaison service for various bilingual communities. The appointments may be through LEAs, the borough services, special posts in community organisations, advice centres, local CREs, mother-tongue classes, or holiday projects, etc.

(c) Related to (b) above are those voluntary workers and activists in community organisations who are willing to liaise with homes, represent family concerns to schools, and interpret aspects of the educational service to the community. This type of liaison or outreach is extremely important because it is independent from the LEA. It is a service that schools and the LEA should be able and willing to pay for.

(d) Finally there is the important option of making special appointments to undertake the outreach and liaison role with the various bilingual communities. Those appointed could be school-based, regional or divisional; they could be teacher posts or on some other salary scale; they could work on their own or alongside monolingual teachers. A key issue in these apppointments (as with the appointment of mother-tongue teachers) is that the relevant communities should have a proper voice in the job description, shortlisting, and appointment procedures, because schools are in no position to judge how acceptable individual candidates may be to the communities. Sectors of the educational service which are experienced in the appointment and role of outreach workers are Adult Education and the Youth Service and it could be valuable for the school sector to be involved in more such posts. Clearly these are very responsible posts and it is important that the job should have an appropriate salary level.

The administrative procedures between an LEA office, schools, support services and other agencies should ensure efficient collation and dissemination of appropriate information on bilingual pupils and their families. The procedures should take account of different cultural, religious, and language backgrounds (amendment of forms, cards, etc).

Most LEAs at present rely solely on Educational Welfare Officers for contact with families outside of school. Educational Welfare Officers are by training and by job description restricted to attempting to meet the needs of individual families/children. This is clearly an essential task, but it does not resolve either the difficulties of the community in becoming more organised around educational issues, nor does it provide a mechanism for dissemination of educational information to the community at large. In addition to EWOs, community workers and advice workers could be funded to work for Educational Advice and Support Centres, details of which are proposed below. It is difficult to propose a precise number of posts because that will depend upon the number of centres which are set up, but one can envisage that an absolute minimum of four professional staff would be needed at each Centre.

3.4 Educational Advice and Support Centres

Such centres could be established along these lines:

SUPPORT AND MANAGEMENT
As outlined in earlier paragraphs, the Educational Advice and Support Centres would be funded by the LEA, but will be independent organisations run by a management committee made up of volunteers from community groups, parents, agencies with whom the centre is in contact (including the LEA), etc.

STAFFING AND LOCATION
In order that they are accessible to parents and to all potential users of the education system, there will need to be a number of centres in easily accessible locations (e.g. main shopping areas) and in shop-type premises. Apart from the necessary administrative support there will need to be at least two community workers and two advice workers in each centre.

FUNCTION
(a) To provide a range of services to parents, families and individuals involving information, relevant classes, and general personal support;

(b) to provide representation for pupils, students and parents in their dealings with the education system;

(c) to work with community organisations to disseminate information about the educational services on offer and to assist in the mobilisation and focussing of local demands for improvement in those services;

(d) to draw the schools, parents, community organisations and other agencies into closer partnership by increasing contact and mutual understanding;

(e) to act as a base for bilingual Educational Welfare Officers;

(f) to provide space for education classes, meeting of community organisations, etc;

(g) to provide creche facilities for users of the centre;

(h) to act as a link for all those agencies with an interest in the welfare of children.

Relationships

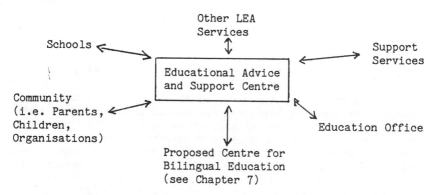

3.5 **Education for all members of the family**

There are two complementary reasons for being concerned with education provision for whole families when required:

(a) All adults have a right to educational opportunity for their own sakes as individual people and as members of our bilingual society. Those people who have only recently come into the area and have very little English at their command are, almost inevitably, less likely to know how to seek and find the education they need, which is likely to include E2L as well as some teaching both of their mother tongues and through the medium of their mother tongues.

(b) As parents keenly interested in their children's welfare and education, they cannot participate in the parental and community influence on the schools or give the detailed support to their children that they would wish if they do not understand sufficiently the organisation of a school or its curriculum.

Family education initiatives can draw parents and children closer together and increase parental partnership with schools in the children's education. Educational Advice and Support services would be ideally placed to offer a range of services to help parents. However, it is unlikely that the needs of families, especially those nenwly arrived from overseas, can be met without a fresh consideration of family education.

3.6 Representation

The call for the black perspective can be seen as a pre-condition for co-operative work in dismantling discriminatory and racist practices in society and in the education system. In the context of promoting bilingual education in schools it will involve the school being directly informed by parents and others to whom bilingualism is part of their daily lives.

It is more than just keeping in touch through letters home in the parents' first language. We must be careful not to use parents' first language as a one-way channel of communication. Whilst supporting various bilingual approaches which enable the school to voice its needs to the parents, equal weight must be given to how a voice is provided for such parents within the school. The EEC "School and Family Conference", which had representatives from parent organisations throughout the EEC as well as educators, called for parents' organisations to "influence educational policy" (Commission of the European Communities, 1983, p.12).

If we are to work effectively we must recognise the low levels of representation of minority ethnic groups on decision-making bodies within the school, e.g. PTAs, PAs, and governing bodies, all of which to a greater or lesser extent tend to reflect the majority white interests. That imbalance must be redressed.

A series of reports have stated that the governing body should reflect the communities it serves, a statement also reinforced by the Rampton Report (Committee of Inquiry, 1981) which called for steps to be taken by LEAs to ensure that minority interests are taken into account in making appointments to the governing bodies of schools.

If we accept that the level of achievement of a bilingual student is in part affected by the status given to bilingualism within the school, it follows that a governing body which includes parent representatives committed to the principle of bilingual education is more likely to develop practices in accordance with those principles. Once again, the perspective of parents from a bilingual background is essential if a school's policy is to be informed by those directly concerned with bilingualism. Such elected parents would ideally be representatives of or have contact with community groups with an interest in bilingualism. This would not only mean that such parents' views would be seen to reflect a wider body of opinion, but would also assist with the dissemination of information between schools, parents, and the community.

The onus is on the school to develop ways to bring about the representation of parents from bilingual backgrounds onto the governing body. One way to achieve this would be to work through the bilingual outreach worker or home-school liaison officer.

One of the recommendations of the Hargreaves Committee was that parents should make up at least one quarter of the governing body and that the governing bodies be increased from 20 to 23, five of which would be parents. Four would be elected by and from the parents in the school and the fifth would be co-opted by the governors to ensure that any minority groups among the parents were represented.

> An improvement in home school relations is of particular importance to ethnic minorities.
> (Committee on the Curriculum and Organisation of Secondary Schools, 1984, p.19)

The 1986 Education Act came to the same conclusion, specifying in schools of more than 599 pupils that there should be as many (five) parent governors as those appointed by the local education authority (DES, 1986, pp. 4-5). ILEA has devised a co-option system for members of minority ethnic communities.

In fact all the decision-making bodies within each school should be examined to ensure that the different language speakers from the community that the school serves are able to express their needs and have some control over the way they are met. To avoid tokenism it is important to recognise the need to appoint more than one member from a minority group.

Access for community groups with a special interest in bilingualism could be facilitated through regular school/community meetings. The recommendations of the group could then be fed through the school decision-making structure. To make such a group truly viable, the different ethnic minorities would have to be represented, and questions of the group's status within the school and accountability would have to be thoroughly debated so as to eliminate any sense of marginalisation, tokenism, or lip-service.

In the context of improved home/school relations, it is important to remind ourselves of the benefit to be derived by the <u>whole</u> school if bilingualism, through parental and community representation, has a significant place within the decision-making structures of the school. Representation of people from minority ethnic and linguistic communities must be seen as an essential part of our efforts to decrease the gulf between home and school and as a move towards a more open education, one in which parents have a greater say in and control over the education of their children.

4   INTO SCHOOL

4.1 Population mobility

Most educational planning (administrative, pastoral, and curriculum) appears to presume a pattern of all children having continuous schooling. They are expected to enter a primary school at five, stay in that school until they transfer, perhaps to a middle school, and then have the remainder of their compulsory education in a single secondary or high school. However, there is considerable population mobility, and in urban areas administrators and schools have to be prepared to receive pupils at all ages.

Children arrive at our schools in a variety of contexts, all of which have particular needs. These contexts include:

(a) starting primary school,

(b) transferring from primary to secondary schools,

(c) entering school at all ages on arrival in Britain from abroad,

(d) transferring schools at all ages on arrival from another part of a local authority, or another part of the country.

It is imperative that we improve the identification, forecasting, placement, and reception of bilingual pupils in the schools, facilitate the transfer of pupils between schools, and ensure that bureaucratic procedures become more responsive to the needs of parents and pupils from different cultural, linguistic, and religious backgrounds. We will consider identification and forecasting procedures in Chapter 7.

4.2 Placement

Every authority has a statutory obligation under the 1944 Education Act to provide appropriate education places for individual pupils. Parents have an equal obligation under the same Act to ensure that their children receive adequate education.

It must be emphasised that parents can exercise choice under the terms of the 1980 Education Act. An authority's admissions policy sets out the criteria upon which places are allocated. Schools must accept pupils where vacancies exist in the appropriate age group beneath the total fixed by the schools' defined "forms of entry". While the admissions criteria at secondary or high school transfer can include the sibling factor, distance from schools (and in the case of some voluntary schools denominational considerations), levels of English language competence are not factors which should be taken into account.

There is evidence in some areas that the placement of bilingual pupils has not been easy because of a number of factors, including the lack of vacancies in many over-subscribed secondary schools, the preference of some families for single-sex girls' schools, the mobility of the local population, schools pleading that they have insufficient E2L teaching resources, the apparent unwillingness of certain schools to accept bilingual students, the inability of entry criteria to recognise the needs of bilingual students, and the racism that occurs both within and around schools.

4.3 Reception

The first contact that many families have with the educational system is when they approach an Education Office or a school to find places for their children. It is therefore of the utmost importance that reception and admission procedures are non-threatening so that the families feel welcome and have the confidence to seek support and advice.

At the Education Office

It is good to see many education offices making their premises welcoming with displays of pupils' work throughout the building on a regularly changing basis and directions given in more than one language. This last move of course involves a careful appointment of receptionists, who should be bilingual, and have ready access to interpreters, on a similar basis to the translators described earlier. All staff should also have access to regular in-service training which will enable them to develop working procedures that are more responsive to the needs and rights of the bilingual families they cater for.

At schools

Schools can maximise the use of the valuable resources already within the school by:

(a) involving bilingual pupils and staff as interpreters and receptionists;

(b)   setting up in secondary schools a welcoming reception area and
        a desk operated by pupils as, for instance, recommended by the
        Hargreaves Committee:

> 3.1.9 One simple method of making the school approachable
> is to provide a reception desk operated by pupils. In
> most schools one or two pupils are free at most times of
> the day, if only because they are excused physical
> education or games. If a desk is placed near the main
> entrance, the pupils can welcome any visitors and direct
> them appropriately. It is also an excellent social
> education for the pupils on reception duty. In a few
> schools we visited, one or two pupils were awaiting our
> arrival and, since we were expected and arrived
> punctually, we were addressed by name - our sense of being
> welcome was immediate and profound.

> (Committee on the Curriculum and Organisation of
> Secondary Schools, 1984, p.15)

Such a system would probably not be viable in primary schools
but parents could be encouraged to participate and organise
reception. This provision would enhance the status, confidence,
and image of all pupils and parents, especially those who are
bilingual.

(c)   displaying attractively in the reception area the School's
        Booklet and samples of work. To help parents and pupils the
        booklets should be readily available in a variety of languages
        with the pages in side-by-side translation.

(d)   establishing clear procedures (of which everyone is aware) for
        helping families who arrive unexpectedly. These procedures
        should include clear guidance to staff about the information
        that should be obtained to be relayed to the appropriate
        department within the school, and to the school-attached EWO,
        and the Bilingual EWO so that advice and help can be given
        where necessary (e.g. re. clothing, free dinners, or links with
        social services).

(e)   providing appropriate in-service training for administration/
        support staff, and sharing the knowledge teachers may have of
        the bilingual pupils and their communities with the office
        staff, who are likely to be the first to meet families seeking
        admission into the school. School secretaries are often
        bewildered by enquiries from minority ethnic families, not just
        because of the language barrier but also because they know so
        little of their backgrounds and circumstances. The more they
        understand about these families, the more appropriate and
        sympathetic their handling of them will be.

Information also needs to flow outwards to the community. Therefore details of reception procedures should be made available to outside agencies such as public libraries, health centres, GP's, Social Services, housing departments, homeless persons units, youth clubs, under-5's facilities, community centres, and supplementary schools.

Both the Education Office and the schools could as an immediate step draw up a directory of their staff who are fluent in a language other than English. In the long term, it would be proper to appoint more bilingual staff, and to offer all staff the opportunity to take a communication course in another language. A further positive move would be to offer staff a short course in cross-cultural communication in order to better understand the families they serve.

4.4 Induction

Ideally each school should offer a planned school-based induction programme. This should include a tour of the buildings for both parents and pupils, and should introduce them to the organisation, curriculum, and ethos of the school. It should also attempt to explain the aims and objectives of the LEA. There is much to be said for offering such a programme to new bilingual pupils _after_ an initial period in school.

When primary or middle school children transfer there is usually a lengthy and planned induction programme and at this stage pupils gain support from one another as they often attended the same primary schools. It is doubly important, therefore, that there is a carefully planned induction programme for bilingual pupils who often arrive as casual admissions with little or no support from a peer group or with little or no experience of school. This is supported again by the Hargreaves Committee which commends those schools in which:

> Pupils with no English at all are given an induction course in the ESL department to familiarise them with the building and a small range of teachers. As their social and linguistic confidence grows, they are gradually moved into the class and year appropriate to them, with the support teacher still occasionally in attendance to ease the transfer process.
> (Committee on the Curriculum and Organisation of Secondary Schools, 1984, 3.7.4, p.46)

During the period of induction into secondary school all bilingual students should attend secondary school full-time. Any attendance at an off-site centre at this critical time would exacerbate any induction problems and would limit important social interactions.

Procedures should be established for inducting not just new children coming into the school but also their families into the working of the authority. The precise strategies for doing this will need considerable discussion, but the induction system should have the following characteristics:

(a) it should involve the whole family and be held at a time suitable for them, but it should not delay children being placed on the roll of the school;

(b) it should be conducted as much as possible through the medium of their home language, and should also utilize slides, tapes or videos;

(c) its aims should be to increase the security and confidence of the pupils and their families, to ensure that they understand the educational options available to them and the role the whole family can play in supporting the educational progress of their children;

(d) it should not function as or be open to interpretation as a way of segregating bilingual children from mainstream education.

4.5 **School transfer**

The transfer from any school to another is difficult but the move from primary or middle to secondary school can be especially traumatic for children who are not fluent in English. They leave the comparative security of a small school where they are usually under the care of one teacher to move to the complex organisation of a secondary or high school where they have to relate to many teachers. In primary, first and middle schools, knowledge about the children, their language skills, their learning strengths and needs is often held by one teacher. In secondary school, that knowledge has to be rediscovered by (or remains hidden among) all the subject teachers. The transfer of comprehensive, unambiguous, accurate information is of great importance to enable the receiving teachers to plan appropriate education. First-stage English learners, in particular, cannot afford to lose learning opportunities while secondary teachers take time to discover skills already developed in primary schools.

The Hargreaves Report identifies good practice for the transition from primary to secondary school (Committee on the Curriculum and Organisation of Schools, 1984, p.24-30). The following points seem particularly relevant to bilingual children:

(a) Records should be supplemented with meetings between teachers. We recommend that meetings about transferring children should be arranged by Divisional Office. These meetings should involve fourth year junior teachers, EWOs, a teacher from each secondary school (e.g. head of first year), bilingual EWOs.

(b) The information received in secondary school should be disseminated among subject teachers. We recommend the model of a 'form meeting', chaired by the tutor and involving all subject teachers.

(c) Portfolios of children's work should be passed on from primary to secondary school.

(d) Secondary teachers should visit primary schools in order, amongst other things, to plan for curriculum-continuity and to see for themselves how the children work and how they are taught.

(e) There should be a carefully planned induction programme (including points (a) to (d) above) which should cover the final half-year in junior school and the first half-year in secondary school. This induction programme should be the responsibility of an identified person in each secondary school.

Parents of bilingual children are often unaware of the transfer procedures and of the choices open to them. Positive steps should be taken to remedy this. A Bilingual Education Welfare Officer should be responsible for access to this information.

It is important for secondary schools to receive useful and accurate information for each student. For first and second stage learners, this information should include:

(a) some details of linguistic ability in the first language;

(b) some details of mathematical ability (gained, if possible, using an oral practical test in the first language);

(c) some indication of their fluency in English and of the kinds of tasks they can be expected to succeed in using English as the medium.

Any testing of bilingual children should offer the opportunity to be tested in the mother tongue.

5   TEACHING AND LEARNING

5.1   Introduction

As has been argued, the administrative, reception, induction, and overall organisational arrangements for schools must be substantially adjusted if proper educational provision is to be made for all students, the bilingual as well as those who speak only English. At the heart of our concern, obviously, is the teaching and learning. It is clear that there has been insufficient national or local debate about the opportunities for teaching and learning with bilingual students. Indeed, the educational discussion has virtually always been framed only in terms of 'their' need to learn English. The response to this debate was then seen as singular: provide English tuition and 'they' would fit into the school system as it stood.

This narrow focus on bilingual students' need to learn English has, in effect if not by intent, marginalised the needs, concerns, and voice of those students and the communities they represent:

(a)   It assumes that students need access only to English and thus fails to recognise their right and continuing need to operate and develop the languages of their own communities and cultural heritage; our teaching should recognise that many parts of our country are and always will be multilingual societies.

(b)   It offers native fluency in English alone as the recipe for all levels of access and success and fails to recognise how racism operates as a barrier to learning. Education should support our students and their communities in their struggle for equality of opportunity.

(c)   It presupposes that language and culture are separable, and by focussing on English in a vacuum fails to recognise the role of the students' first language and culture in their learning. Our teaching should reflect and celebrate, not exclude, the diverse cultures of our students.

It is therefore necessary to add other layers to the debate about the language development needs of bilingual students, including their right to learn in and through their first or home language. To create a full education for bilingual students is not merely to add "E2L" in the early stages, nor even to be more thoughtful and add "mother tongue"; it must be to re-consider the whole curriculum and create a coherent pattern of teaching and learning that will retain and develop the students' own language and culture, whilst at the same time helping her or him to develop fully in the whole range of subjects, and to be able to move between languages in a variety of intellectual as well as occupational and social contexts. Meeting the learning needs of bilingual students means more than simply arranging for specialist language help. To offer equality of opportunity to bilingual learners and their families and eliminate the racism that is amplified by language difference, changes which affect the whole curriculum are needed.

5.2. Pupil needs and teaching goals

The richness of the linguistic diversity in the country's schools means that we are helping a range of young people to learn whose language patterns vary from English mother tongue to monolingual speakers of other languages, with a vast number and range of combinations.

The common stereotype of bilingual pupils as unable to make much use of English (thus dubbed "E2L pupils") masks the continuum of competence in two or more languages and the relative strengths and functions of these languages to the young person and her or his family, strengths and functions which are different in many cases between members of the family. Indeed, the dominance of the standard phrase "E2L" itself confuses the status of a number of bilingual pupils for whom English may be second (or third) in chronological order of learning, but actually first in current strength. As one second-year secondary boy put it: 'My first language was Armenian, because that's what my mother spoke to me when I was a baby; my home language is Farsee; but the language I speak best is English.'

Such pupils have been bilingual all their lives, and bring to a school a very powerful linguistic richness. They have a great deal to offer.

(a) In English, it is likely they need sophisticated advanced teaching, well beyond the normal level of E2L classes in schools, but different in some content and structure from the usual subject "English" lessons, especially in terms of the consciousness of the working of language.

(b) Alongside this they should be offered the opportunity to choose which of their "home" or "community" languages they and their parents wish to develop as their second strongest language.

Whether children speak hardly a word of English because they have only recently arrived in this country, or they speak fluent English at age five, they will have certain linguistic and educational needs which it is the job of the education authority to meet - or, at minimum, to ensure are met in combination with external agencies. In particular,we would stress the right of all children to education in the subject areas, even when they do not yet speak or write English.

In discussing educational provision for bilingual pupils, this paper will highlight the special needs of two categories of pupils: those who are "late arrivals" in the school system (see Chapter 6); and those who finish primary or middle school and enter secondary school with low-level literacy skills.

Educational Principles and Rights

In defining pupil needs, therefore, it is first imperative to lay down certain principles which should officially be recognised as a guide to practical initiatives at the earliest possible moment. It is the right of every child of school age (and beyond) to:

(a) receive instruction adequate to enable him or her to speak, read, and write English;

(b) receive instruction adequate to enable her or him to speak, read, and write her or his mother tongue (which may, of course, be English);

(c) have equal access to all education opportunities;

(d) be educated in an environment where all cultures are given equal respect;

(e) be given an understanding of his or her cultural heritage, and also taught to have a sympathy for and access to other people's cultures - and thus to acquire intercultural understanding;

(f) determine, with her or his family and community, preferred choices within the whole-school curriculum.

How those rights are achieved

The right to fluency and literacy in English at present is granted automatically only to English mother-tongue speakers, i.e. the English language resources available in schools are overwhelming for English mother-tongue speakers. There is, therefore, a need for massive relocation of resources if those who are bilingual are to be given equality of access to English. There is also a need for structured support, which should not be confused with remedial help: you cannot remedy something that has not gone wrong!

The right to speak, read, and write in an individual's own mother tongue implies the need for:

66

(a) the opportunity to use and develop the first language in a variety of contexts and for a variety of purposes. Schools will therefore need to consider how they can provide scope for the students in academic, pastoral, and social contexts;

(b) an audience for both speech and writing. It is not possible to develop appropriate language skills without authentic communication, and students therefore require regular contact with both peers and adults who share their mother tongue;

(c) support in terms of both personnel and materials resources.

Of course equality does not mean the same. The measurement of equality has to be gauged by results achieved, not just by the resources put in, i.e. for those, who for one reason or another are disadvantaged, additional resources will be required to provide equality of opportunity. Equality of access can be a reality only if all children can understand what is being taught (formal or informal), i.e. there is a need for interpreters, translators, mother-tongue speakers, English language support, and appropriate materials, as well as a need to assess overall curriculum content. There must be freedom from racial harrassment, and schools must develop a positive anti-racist policy. All activities must take account of different cultural traditions. There must be a development of language awareness for all pupils. The relationship between school and community must allow bilingual parents equal access, equal understanding - and equal consultation, i.e. equal power.

5.3 Curriculum models

Introduction

"Bilingualism" means being reasonably skilled in the use of more than one language. At present, however, state education in Britain is planned for all students as monolingual. Because the UK curriculum has in the past been so Euro-centric and because of the historical dominance of French in the languages curriculum, together with the country's general disparagement of "foreign" languages and the slight impact of language teaching generally, bilingual education is a new concept to many people both in education and outside it. Such steps as have been taken have tended to be seen as "compensatory" for "immigrants", and have been limited to helping them in the early stages of their education, with little gained by other members of the school and little long-term development. There has been fragmentation, with splits between "E2L", "Foreign Languages", "Mother Tongue" (in a few cases only), and the rest of the curriculum. Even the most hard-working schools have tended to keep these aspects separate, and to see one mode of organisation as the only way of working. Many modes (such as the importance at certain stages of teaching content through the medium of the pupil's strongest language) have frequently been suppressed as being "divisive" or not forcing students to learn English quickly enough.

What is advocated by researchers like Wright (1982) is a series of developmental models which indicate the transitional stages which schools and their communities might adopt in a progressive movement towards the establishment of a fully biliterate bilingual approach (Wright, 1982, p.13). These models, described in Appendix A, suggest a spectrum of responses to the needs of a multilingual society from the early stages whereby mother tongues are used only as a springboard for the future development of proficiency in English to the more sophisticated approaches which culminate in both languages having equal status as the medium of instruction and expression. The models can be summed up here by describing two basic patterns for curriculum provision: one we should regard as minimal and the other as extended, which should be an option open to parents and students.

The minimal or basic model

At the very least this should offer students for whom English is not their first language the opportunities:

(a) to gain sufficient command of English to be able to take their place in all English-speaking situations, personal, social, educational, and occupational, as they may wish;

(b) to have the benefit of pastoral care and guidance to the same extent as English mother-tongue speakers;

(c) to attain as well in the full range of subjects in the curriculum as English mother-tongue speakers;

(d) to develop their control of their mother tongue at least for personal and social purposes within their own community;

(e) to learn of the culture and literature of their first language.

This model goes further than what is technically called the "subtractive" approach to bilingual education (Lambert, 1977), as it, in (d) and (e), insists on some development of the language and culture of the pupil's heritage. We cannot condone a merely "subtractive" approach, which is sometimes called "transitional bilingual education", and seeks to replace the first language by that of the majority language (Wright, 1982, p.9). However, to offer only the minimal model we have described would be inadequate for many of the important aims we set out in Chapter 2 (especially

2.7): it would not offer students the possibility of fully developed bilingualism for their adult lives, nor would it make available to the country bilingual speakers. This requires there to be available as an option to families and students at a further stage:

The extended model

For students who have advanced sufficiently in their English to be able to benefit genuinely from English-medium subject teaching and pastoral care, the minimal model would propose little more than "mother-tongue maintenance" - a very limited concept. However, these are the students who have the possibility of operating equally effectively in both languages in all contexts and for all purposes: informally, socially, for higher education, and professionally. This would require:

(a) development of the mother tongue in a way analogous to the teaching of English to English mother-tongue students;

(b) continuation of E2L beyond the stage at which too often tuition is withdrawn because the student can now "get by", analogous to the advanced second-language teaching to English mother-tongue students;

(c) most important, and possibly most controversially, the teaching of some "subjects" through the medium of the student's mother tongue. There is little hope of full development in a language if its use is restricted to social occasions and its teaching to "language" lessons: stretching intellectual assignments are required. Thus options should be available for some of the 16-plus examinations to be taught and examined in and through the student's mother tongue, e.g. literature, history, or social studies;

(d) a variety of "extra-curriculum" meetings, journeys, lectures giving a range of mother-tongue experiences.

It will be noticed that "subject teaching" (which includes both the secondary and the primary curricula), in the medium of the student's first language is proposed at the two extremes:

(a) for English beginners, because only thus can they get access to the curriculum for an initial period;

(b) for advanced bilingual students, because only thus can both their languages be fully developed.

The first could be seen as "transitional", and the second would be true biliterate bilingualism, and genuinely prestigious.

5.4 Teaching patterns

Modes of provision

The curriculum models described have to be translated into teaching
patterns, into subjects taught through one or more languages.   The
components of these patterns are simple to list:

> teaching in English
> teaching of English
> teaching in mother tongue
> teaching of mother tongue.

The matrix that follows is an attempt to set out different types of
teaching provision that are used or could be used in order to
achieve our two related objectives:

(a) to give bilingual pupils effective and rapid access to the
     mainstream curriculum, and to facilitate their successful
     integration into the English-speaking peer group;

(b) to promote their bilingualism by developing their command of
     English and of the language of their home or community (the
     abbreviation 'MT' is used here).

These two objectives, as already argued, are not mutually exclusive
alternatives.   Rather they are the end points of a scale which
allows teaching and learning activities to be described according to
whether their objective is primarily:

> (A) language development (English or MT),

or primarily   (B) the understanding of or access to the mainstream
               curriculum,

> or (A/B) some combination of the two.

This scale is the horizontal axis of the matrix.   The vertical axis
is also a scale, describing which language is the medium of
instruction.   This scale has the teaching medium exclusively mother
tongue at one end and exclusively English at the other.   In between
there are various possible combinations or balances between the two
languages.   Each type of teaching or learning provision within the
framework is further described by identifying the types of teacher
likely to be involved and whether the bilingual learners are likely
to be withdrawn from their regular classes or not.   In describing
the type of teacher likely to be involved, the term "bilingual"
defines teachers who speak the same community language as the
bilingual pupils.   The terms "mainstream" or "E2L" teacher includes
teachers who are bilingual in the same language as the pupils,
although the majority of such teachers will not share the languages
of the pupils.

	THE CONSCIOUS FOCUS OR MAIN GOAL OF THE LESSON		
TEACHING MEDIUM	A. LANG. DEVELOPMENT Oracy and Literacy	AB. LANG. DEVELOPMENT AND CURRICULUM CONTENT	B. UNDERSTANDING OF/ ACCESS TO CURRICULUM
MT	1/ Special lessons to learn MT, reading, writing 16+ & A-level Usually withdrawal.	2/ Special classes for MT learning but through medium of topics and subject areas. NB. The current role and contribution of Community MT classes.	3/ General lessons taught by bilingual teachers using MT. eg. initial access infant classes or subject teaching at sec. level. (NB especially, cultur- ally significant subjects such as MT literature.)
Predominantly MT with English support.	4/ As above but with the teacher using English as an alternative medium for teaching as and when necessary. Use of English MT dictionaries to explore meanings of words that are new in MT.		
Equal balance between MT and English	5/ Lessons such as story telling first in MT then in English Mainsteam or Withdrawal	6/ Maths lesson team taught by bilingual and monolingual – Equal roles – usually mainstream	
Predominantly English with MT support	7/ As below but using one or more of the following strategies to support through MT: a) bilingual teachers – team teaching b) bilingual classroom assistants c) bilingual peers – classroom cooperation d) bilingual older pupils – cross-age tutoring e) parents and other members of community – groups assignments f) bilingual materials – speech and text.		
English	8/ Separate E2L Groups focusing on forms, structures & other specific aspects of English. Bilinguals in Main- stream lessons where some aspect of English language is the focus.	9/ Separate E2L Groups learning English through topics and appropriate curriculum areas. Mainstream lessons involving topics/ subject areas but with language learn- ing objectives considered and integrated.	10/ Bilinguals in mainstream lesson focus on participating in project-topic or subject area.

Key to Modes of Provision: The Spectrum of Possibilities

Types of Teacher involved

```
1/       Teacher:  bilingual
         Mode:     usually withdrawal or subject option at upper
                   secondary level

2/       Teacher:  bilingual
         Mode:     usually withdrawal

3/       Teacher:  bilingual
         Mode:     usually withdrawal

4/       Teacher:  bilingual
         Mode:     usually withdrawal

5/       Teacher:  (a) bilingual or
                   (b) bilingual and monolingual together
& 6/     Mode:     (a) mainstream or withdrawal
                   (b) mainstream

7/       Teacher:  E2L or mainstream with bilingual teacher or
                   other bilingual support strategy
         Mode:     usually mainstream

8/ & 9/ (a) Teacher:  E2L
            Mode:     Withdrawal

        (b) Teacher:  Mainstream (English subject)
            Mode:     Usually mainstream
```

English as a Second Language

The phrase "English as a Second Language" brings to most people's minds a separate class of E2L pupils engaged in the main activity of learning English as a language, that is without a content context. Similarly, the idea of the "mother-tongue" classes suggests a pure language activity to most people. There will be times when pupils will require just that, but it is important to recognise the doubts of many about such separate, language-orientated lessons as being sufficient or even the most appropriate for more than a few learning stages. For instance, in the very early stages of a pupil's time in a school, if she or he has virtually no ability to understand English, some separate English lessons with pupils of a similar level must be beneficial, especially in the secondary subject-based curriculum. Even, though, when such separate E2L lessons are judged

72

appropriate, it is important that the pupils have a proportion of lessons in the subject classes (possibly with mother-tongue aides or mother-tongue teachers) and in such early stages it is likely that certain subjects will require at least some teaching of the subject through the medium of the pupil's strongest language. Conversely, it might be best for older, more advanced students, who can take most of their subject curriculum through the medium of English, to have advanced lessons in English as well to ensure that the flexibility, accuracy, and effectiveness of their English is developed to the highest degree possible. It might be found that a pure English-medium subject curriculum would not do this sufficiently for the able older student aiming at university in the Sciences, for instance.

Mother tongue

Lessons in and through the mother tongue may be advisable as a separate activity for part of the week if, for instance, the pupil is only partially literate in her or his mother tongue, for (as stressed in Section 2.6) growth in English is likely to be better and faster if literacy is developed in the first language. It is unlikely that this mother-tongue tuition should ever be stopped, for without it the mother tongue might be "maintained" but would not be "developed" in the full linguistic range. One could imagine a student opting for one 16+ exam subject in the mother tongue, and then taking the mother tongue again separately as an Advanced Level subject both to extend his or her depth and range in the mother tongue and to add to the portfolio of A-Levels offered for university entrance.

The literature and culture of a particular ethnic group might be taught in English by the specialist bilingual teacher as a module in, say, lower-secondary Humanities for every class (in rotation) in conjunction with the normal subject teacher; mother tongue speakers of that language might also attend community-based or after-school classes with greater coverage and intensity, possibly given by the same teacher. There then might be a specialist Literature option in the fourth- and fifth-years in, say, Bengali or Chinese literature to the sixteen-plus examination. Such options would, of course, be open to both English- mother-tongue and mother-tongue speakers; although in practice few English mother-tongue speakers would opt for such a course, a true bilingual education policy would offer that opportunity, and thus be enriching for those whose first language is English. The flow of students taking up specialized university courses in the community languages would be small, but valuable in three ways: for those individuals given that opportunity, for the adult population of professionals thus added to in shortage subjects, and to the standing of the language in the school and elsewhere.

73

Early Subject Learning

The pupil who arrives with little or no English in a school is effectively denied access to the content of teaching when that teaching is in the medium of English.

The most recent British survey reports:

> There was little support among the majority of authorities for teaching children of minority ethnic group origin at secondary stage other subjects in their mother tongue because there is considered to be no real educational need and no demand from the communities, because the practical difficulties would be considerable and because there are other more pressing priorities. Six authorities expressed support or considered the idea worth investigating: 'we think this is important throughout but especially (a) at the start of formal education, (b) in secondary subject areas'; 'this authority would be sympathetic provided that ... funds were provided for the employment of these teachers and teachers could be found to cope with fifteen different languages of pupils in the authority's schools'. Other authorities who were unsympathetic about use of mother tongue in this way at secondary stage said that it could be important at the nursery and primary stages, particularly to assist concept development and identity.
> (Little and Willey, 1981, p.21)

However, the report goes on to recommend action "to assess the benefits and practical difficulties involved in providing ... other subjects in minority ethnic groups' mother tongues" (ibid, p.33).

Access to mother-tongue learning can theoretically be through the variety of modes described:

(a) bilingual teachers (i) team teaching or (ii) special classes;

(b) bilingual instructors - team teaching;

(c) bilingual peers - classroom co-operation;

(d) bilingual older pupils - cross-age tutoring;

(e) parents and other members of the community - home assignments, community education link-up.

Variations

The various modes of teaching and learning have all been used in

74

various schools in the UK or in other countries with bilingual education. A judicious choice has to be made according to the age of the pupils, the extent of language development, the organisation of the school, the resources and expertise available, and the combination of pupils. However, rarely or never should one of the modes be used in a school on its own, as a number of patterns are possible combining different modes, often in ways by which one mode complements another. Thus, a secondary school judging that pupils with little knowledge in English will have their science taught in mainstream classes with bilingual aides, may still consider it wise to give a pre-science course for a few weeks through the mother tongue to help the pupils prepare for and make the best use of the new subject when they are introduced to this. Such a course could be on the timetable, after normal school hours, or in the holidays as part of a pre-term induction course.

Across schools

Again, the patterns chosen by particular schools might well be complemented by across-school arrangements, particularly for languages with small numbers of speakers in any one school. One could imagine on-the-timetable mother-tongue teaching of large-number minority languages in a school (at whatever levels and in whatever combinations) being supplemented by lessons in a language such as Tagalog or Yoruba at LEA Centres for Bilingual Education (see Chapter 7). Certain clusters of schools might similarly make across-school arrangements for primary story-telling, secondary literature options, or Advanced-Level language work. It is feasible that the repertoire of patterns should be exploited in a variety of combinations.

Individual study packs

The ILEA, for instance, has a strong tradition in science education of solving the problem of very small numbers of students in certain categories in any one school and in certain cases of shortages of specialist and well qualified teachers by using individual learning packages (e.g. Ilpac for A-Level Chemistry). Some aspects of bilingual learning (e.g. literature) and some mother-tongue work in languages with low numbers (e.g. Tigrinyan, Tagalog, Amharic, Yoruba, and other African languages) could be carried out with the help of such study packs. It is possible to see them being used in combination with all the other modes described.

Criteria for choice

Each school and cluster of schools and LEA Centres for Bilingual

75

Education will of course have to make choices of modes and combinations of modes, though these choices are not in their essential nature at all different from the curriculum decisions that schools are obliged to make for any other aspect of the curriculum. In considering these choices, schools will no doubt be concerned with:

(a) the number of the languages spoken and of the speakers of each language;

(b) the linguistic features and the world and cultural position of that language;

(c) the language-development stage of the pupils in that language;

(d) the stage in English which the pupils have reached;

(e) the resources available in terms of number of teachers, aides, and other professionals, as well as the training, skills, and qualifications that they and the English-mother-tongue speakers possess;

(f) the wishes of the parents and local communities;

(g) the wishes of the pupils themselves;

(h) the overall educational needs of the pupil, his or her ambitions, and the need to prepare students appropriately for higher education and employment;

(i) the overall curriculum planning of the school and the value of bilingual education even for monolingual English mother-tongue pupils.

The mixture of these and other criteria will not only vary from school to school, but also from time to time. Large schools will be able to offer fourth-year options that can not be managed in some smaller schools as will sixth form or tertiary colleges. Some of the modes already have conventional resourcing (e.g. if a subject in a minority language or the language itself is put into a fourth-year option scheme or a sixth-form curriculum there is absolutely no extra staffing cost). Others require a more flexible use of present resources, but no addition. Some will require an extension and a clearer staffing formula (e.g. mother tongue). But in all cases it should be stressed that the curriculum decisions of matching pupils' needs to resources and organisational patterns is very similar indeed to that ordinarily carried out in devising a curriculum within a school and devising a timetable to embody that curriculum.

So it can be seen that a whole authority (and within that a whole-school) bilingual education policy enriches the education for all. Not only gives the access to the curriculum that equality requires for bilingual pupils, but also opens up vistas of bilingual adults for the future. The key is for each school to utilise the full range of modes of teaching and learning in judiciously chosen combinations.

5.5   Integration/withdrawal

Mixed-ability, multicultural, multilingual classrooms are very complex places, and the expertise and knowledge needed to work within them often seems out of reach of even the most skilled and experienced teachers. Up-to-date knowledge of subject content is needed. So is an understanding of how to set assignments that are challenging yet accessible. To organise space and time for learners to develop their thinking, teachers also need a specialist awareness of language development.

Few teachers at present know all this from within their own experience, and so the argument for "special provision" for learners - "disruptive", "semi-literate", or "remedial" - seems very strong. Withdrawal provision fits well with the need of mainstream teachers "to get on with their normal work" and has the hidden value of putting to one side the thorny problem of how far we as teachers are able to accept and then engineer the changes necessary to make classrooms better learning environments for everyone.

The debate about how best to support the learning of bilingual students thus comes to us as a question about whether or not to withdraw the learners from the mainstream of schooling for separate E2L lessons. Most E2L teaching in UK schools has been based, and to an extent still is based, on the principle of withdrawing children from their regular classes in order to teach them English. The need for withdrawal is argued on the grounds that most mainstream classrooms are, for bilingual learners, places of incomprehension, isolation, and at worst racism.

Although there have been advantages in this strategy, the argument slides over the fact that special language classes can be equally poor places of learning, where neither the teachers nor the students have access to a wide enough curriculum and, socially, both teachers and students can be isolated. The act of separating pupils off in this way has also been described as racist, and certainly the removal of E2L learners from the mainstream encourages the view that they are not the responsibility of subject teachers.

Unfortunately, in many schools at present bilingual pupils do not learn effectively either in their mainstream lessons or in special training groups. This is because mainstream teachers lack E2L training and because E2L teachers lack knowledge of the different subject areas. But there is a growing concern to develop approaches and styles of teaching that will enable bilingual E2L learners to be taught in the mainstream with E2L teachers going into mainstream classes instead of these pupils coming out of the classes.

There is nothing intrinsically racist about withdrawing pupils to give them extra teaching support. The important principle is that schools have an essentially integrated and integrating approach to the education of bilingual pupils with E2L needs, in which every member of the teaching staff recognises and accepts their full role.

Thus ideally most bilingual pupils should attend mainstream classes for the majority of the weekly timetable. This is essential if these pupils are to have access to the whole curriculum, since E2L teachers alone cannot cover this. Moreover current knowledge about the processes of language and learning development indicates that bilingual students, like all other students, need to follow the mainstream curriculum in mixed-ability classes where talk and interaction are central to the learning and teaching that goes on. In addition the growth of understanding between different ethnic groups is more likely to occur where such integration takes place.

Such integration has implications for how learning is organised in our classrooms:

(a) all teachers must accept responsibility for the language development and learning of bilingual pupils;

(b) teaching should give pupils the opportunities to learn through using language (including mother tongues) in discussion, and should not be dominated by teacher talk;

(c) all teachers will need collaborative support in classrooms so that E2L specialists can assist bilingual pupils;

(d) centrally produced materials and resources should be available to teachers;

(e) teaching should give access to mother-tongue learning through a variety of routes:

    i)   bilingual teachers or instructors team teaching;
    ii) bilingual peers or older pupils - classroom co-operation;
    iii) bilingual materials - in speech (cassettes, talking page etc.) and in text.

Each of the above proposals has advantages and disadvantages, and the balance of the advantages is likely to vary according to the age of pupils, the learning activity, the content, and the number of pupils at various language levels.

In order to attain the goals referred to above, there is a strong case for "workshops" for those pupils who are complete beginners in learning English or who have very little literacy in their mother tongue. The "workshops" should be situated in the school (rather than off-site) so that bilingual pupils are not completely cut off from the life of the school, and so that E2L or mother-tongue teachers can monitor their progress in mainstream lessons. The "workshops" would provide the opportunity for the most effective learning, and would concentrate on:

(a) the emotional growth and security of pupils;

(b) the maintenance of and development of literacy in mother tongue. This would show that value is given to mother tongue;

(c) development of important subject concepts in or through mother tongue;

(d) the early stages of E2L and the development of literacy in English.

A programme leading towards equality should not presume the same pupil groupings throughout. There will be a few times when pupils of a similar linguistic heritage would need to be together for certain sessions. Indeed respect for the languages and cultures of others must allow opportunities for those to flourish as the dominant aspect of certain meetings. The various communities will wish to have events and occasions at which the English speaker is the stranger, rather than all occasions being English-dominant. There are after all single-sex schools, and in mixed schools and colleges the concept of providing some separated (but not streamed) classes and discussion groups for girls is gaining acceptance. There will be occasions when schools will wish to develop similar initiatives in regard to community language groups. There will also be occasions, especially in the early years of learning English, when special E2L groups are an advantage.

5.6   Literacy skills

Bilingual pupils may enter our education system at any age from five to fifteen. Those who do not start at the beginning of primary school here will have had varied educational experiences in their own countries. Some have attended high status academic institutions and have achieved a good standard of education in their own language. Others, however, have had only a year or two of primary education at poorly equipped rural schools where they have not mastered even basic literacy skills. All bilingual pupils coming into our education system after the first year of primary school are at a disadvantage, because they have to learn English before being able to participate fully in the learning process. But different pupils face different degrees of difficulty, according to the age they come, the language they speak, and the schools they have previously attended. On the whole, children from other European countries who can read and write in a language that uses the Roman script are likely to make more rapid progress than children who speak a language radically different from English and have to learn a new script. However, the bilingual pupils who face the greatest difficulties are those with limited literacy skills in their mother tongue. They normally take much longer than their peers to acquire literacy in English and are more likely to fail in the British education system.

There are two main categories of such pupils. First, there are pupils who arrive in England from overseas at secondary age having had only a minimal education in their own language. As explained earlier, the process of learning to read and write in English is much more difficult for children who lack a solid educational background, especially when they also have to learn from scratch other skills (such as numeracy, visual perception, etc.) which are required in secondary school and taken for granted among most eleven year olds. Secondly, there are bilingual pupils who have attended the upper forms of primary schools in this country and have gained a fairly fluent grasp of spoken English, but have acquired limited skills in reading and writing. Such pupils are often virtually illiterate in their mother tongue, perhaps because where they lived the age for starting school is later than in England. (For instance, in Morocco children do not go to school until they are seven.)

There is always a danger that lack of competence in English may be confused with lack of intelligence, and it is especially important to avoid this pitfall in the case of pupils from non-English-speaking homes. Whatever the reasons for pupils failing to acquire literacy skills, teachers must be chary of dismissing such pupils as unintelligent just because until they become confident users of written as well as spoken English they will be unable to succeed in our school system.

Bilingual pupils who cannot read or write can gain little from the school curriculum. Even when such children have begun to speak English they do not gain much of educational value from many lessons, because a certain standard in reading and writing is expected by teachers. They fall behind their English-speaking peers week by week and they are likely to end up in Year 5 with no exam passes and no hope of getting qualifications. As they continue through school, their failure may breed disillusionment and resentment against a system which has let them down. Some pupils may even become disruptive and start to truant. Hence the problems posed by their underachievement are not just educational but also social.

Of all the bilingual pupils we teach, schools have most difficulty in meeting the needs and providing an adequate education for those with low-level literacy skills. There are various reasons for this, but the main problem is that the schools are not geared to providing the compensatory programme required by pupils who have not had a full primary education. In many countries from which these pupils come, entry to a particular year of the education system does not depend on age, but in Britain pupils are rigidly grouped with their peers according to their birth dates. This structure hinders a flexible response to pupils who may need time to acquire linguistic and literacy skills. The lack of mother-tongue classes within the school curriculum also works most forcibly against those pupils with literacy problems who would particularly benefit from teaching in their own languages and are at a special disadvantage in having to operate from the outset in English. Such pupils will learn to speak English much faster than they learn to read in the language, and their reading levels may continue to remain well below those of English mother-tongue pupils receiving tuition from the remedial department. Thus their presence in mainstream classes adds a new dimension to the concept of mixed-ability teaching and places severe demands on all classroom teachers.

It is not only the subject teachers who are ill-equipped to teach bilingual pupils with low-level literacy skills. Often E2L teachers and remedial teachers are comparably bemused, because their training does not prepare them for this task. Although E2L and remedial departments have different functions and should be distinct, in this area their work overlaps. For the E2L teaching provided for these pupils will have to be concerned with teaching the mechanics of reading and writing, as much as with teaching the language. Yet, on the one hand, the majority of courses in E2L for secondary level do not include adequate training in the teaching of literacy skills, since literacy is assumed; while on the other hand, in the training of remedial teachers it is assumed that pupils will be learning to read in the mother tongue. An added frustration is the lack of available teaching resources. Because pupils are assumed to be literate in E2L classes and because they are assumed to be native speakers of English in remedial classes, commercially published materials are often quite unsuitable for those pupils who fall into the special category of bilingual learners with low-level literacy skills.

Many of the suggestions made here have relevance to these pupils, but in view of the special and serious difficulties they face it is important to stress the following:

(a) Low-level literacy skills should be recognised as a factor in allocating mother-tongue and E2L teachers to schools, and in establishing the size of E2L "workshops".

(b) Mother-tongue classes with an orientation towards developing literacy skills should be available within the school curriculum as required.

(c) Bilingual pupils with literacy problems would benefit more than any other group from mother-tongue support in mainstream lessons, and from studying some of the curriculum subjects through the mother tongue.

(d) The initial training of E2L and mother-tongue teachers should include adequate preparation for the teaching of literacy skills. In-service training in the teaching of bilingual pupils with low-level literacy skills should be available for all teachers.

(e) Appropriate teaching materials for this category of pupil should be prepared for use in ILEA schools.

5.7 Pastoral care

Many schools are rightly proud of the "pastoral care" that they offer their pupils. Secondary schools have carefully worked out responsibility structures in an effort to ensure that each pupil is served by a team of teachers, with the tutor as the closest and the most frequent support. In primary first or middle schools the class teacher, supported by the headteacher, has a similar aspect to his or her work. "Pastoral care" is the "personal, educational, and vocational guidance" of the pupil, and part of this involves discipline and welfare, including working with "the welfare network" to enable social services, educational welfare officers, and agencies of various sorts to offer the pupil and her or his family access to the educational and social services which are their right. The aspects of pastoral care concerned with links with homes were considered in Chapters 3 and 4. Here we consider the personal, educational, and vocational guidance of pupils within the school.

Although the highest hopes of schools' pastoral care schemes are not always fulfilled, primary class teachers and secondary tutors and form teachers usually know their pupils very well indeed, and formally or informally offer a great deal of guidance. Many pupils turn to their early days of a new school as to how to do this or that; for support if they are unhappy because of difficulties with another pupil or a teacher; to take them into their confidence about personal or family matters that are concerning them; to ask their advice about option choices; and so on. Some of the day-to-day responsibilities of tutors could appear to the casual observer as fairly trivial: checking punctuality, reprimanding for minor misbehaviour, perhaps checking clothing or uniform, ensuring that the pupil has the right books and equipment for the lessons of the day in a secondary school. However, it is through these routine tasks that the tutor or class teachers builds up the knowledge and relationship onto which the more individual and personal guidance can be grafted. This relationship involves many private conversations with the pupil, some on everyday, even light-hearted, matters, but others necessarily involving deep personal exchanges of views, virtually professional counselling. As the standard handbook on tutoring puts it:

> The principal contribution that (the tutor) makes to the group and to its members is his own person.
>   (Blackburn, 1975, p.212)

Medium of discussion

Not all the guidance is individual. Neither the junior school class teacher nor the secondary school tutor, however hard-working, can have the time to give adequate guidance one-to-one. More than that, the skilful teacher uses group discussion to strengthen the guidance work by bringing the spoken contributions of all the group to bear on opportunities and problems. Thus much good secondary school pastoral care is group guidance through the medium of discussion.

Without good pastoral care, especially in the secondary school, the pupil will inevitably find it very difficult or impossible to make good use of the educational opportunities available. "Personal, educational, and vocational guidance" ranges from how to handle homework, through subject-option choice, to enabling the student to make wise post-sixteen decisions. The student denied pastoral care is denied the maps or keys that allow her or him to exercise the students' rights and to shape his or her education.

Although a primary or middle-school class teacher or a secondary tutor can establish a definite rapport with a pupil who so far speaks very little English, and although a few aspects of this personal pastoral care can take place without a language medium, it is difficult to believe that true guidance can be possible without not merely a language exchange but quite a subtle fluency. Clearly "personal, educational, and vocational guidance" must depend on mutual trust and on full, accurate, and sensitive verbal communication. Bluntly, adequate pastoral care by definition cannot be given by a class teacher or tutor incapable of speaking the language of the pupil.

Special guidance

Additionally there are also certain pastoral responsibilities that are particular to certain minority-language speaking pupils such as the translation of official letters, queries about nationality status, and sometimes the tendency of younger pupils with little English in secondary schools to seek shelter away from the sometimes baffling mainstream classes. A serious challenge is that pupils of minority language groups often suffer, in school or on the way to school, various forms of racial harrassment. Although a good tutorial programme would wish to make this a feature of the whole tutor-group discussion as part of the school's anti-racist policy, although the group support can be helpful for the victims, and although such discussions are important for all the pupils, there may be a need for private discussion of these and any other challenges particular to a certain language group. A spokesperson for one Bengali-speaking community, for instance, praised the value of Bangladeshi pupil discussion groups in the lunch time. We remember that many schools have instituted girls groups for similar purposes - that is to provide a forum in which a group of pupils facing particular challenges may discuss them freely without the risk of ridicule or feeling inhibited, and can help each other find ways of helping themselves through group discussion.

Finally, let us eradicate the fear that many teachers may subconsciously develop lower expectations of their bilingual pupils based on the difficulties that they have communicating fully with them. For instance, many third-stage learners tend to achieve below their potential especially in subjects in which the English language is especially important. This needs to be compensated not only by in-service work for tutors and class teachers, but also by special encouragement for the pupils.

For all these reasons and because of their closeness to bilingual pupils, pastoral care for them in secondary schools has often become largely the responsibility of the E2L teacher, whose involvement with and concern for the pupil is so much greater. Such teachers have offered a great deal of help, and in secondary schools are usually trusted by the pupils and parents perhaps more than other teachers. However, if the pupils' or the parents' command of English is limited, there is no doubt that the pastoral care offered is still not as good as that enjoyed by an English-speaking pupil. Further, the E2L teacher in the secondary school often cannot properly become part of the school's pastoral structure.

Clearly, then, on the one hand many bilingual pupils have special additional needs in pastoral care, and on the other hand the mono-lingual tutor cannot adequately offer even the ordinary pastoral care because of her or his language limitations. These points would appear to suggest some separation of pastoral care for pupils whose

English is still elementary. Certainly some School Boards in the USA would regard it as necessary to give such pupils separate "homerooms" (the nearest equivalent to our tutor group) and counsellors who speak the pupil's language. Yet we should be reluctant to take pupils whose mother tongue is not English out of their normal primary classes or secondary tutor groups for much of the week, as they benefit in a variety of important ways from being part of their peers' main social and guidance group, and their presence can be valuable for the other pupils. <u>However, to push this principle of "integration" so far that the pupils receive inadequate pastoral care would be desperately unfair.</u>

The nation has a new emphasis on social and personal education (indeed it is one of the six first priorities of the Schools Curriculum Development Committee) and many schools are proud of their pastoral care; it cannot be denied, however, that bilingual pupils who so far have little English are being denied this aspect of their right to education in the present conditions.

To meet these needs, "complementary tutoring" is required, and the most likely way to provide this would be if an LEA were to recruit, train, and organise (presumably through the Centre for Bilingual Education proposed in Chapter 7) a sufficient number of bilingual pastoral figures, perhaps using the already existing title "Young Person's Adviser", to offer personal guidance and support to bilingual pupils whose English is insufficent to be able to gain this from the class teacher or tutor. These bilingual YPAs could be drawn from the appropriate communities, and would visit their schools on a rota, giving the number of hours required by the number of pupils, and able to meet those pupils individually or in small groups in a suitable room. Pupils could refer themselves or be referred by parents or teachers. We should expect these bilingual YPAs to work closely with the main pastoral structure in secondary schools and with the class teacher in primary schools, not, therefore, so much confidential counsellors as an extension of the school's normal pastoral care approaches.

Although the advice of E2L teachers is sought in schools by tutors, they should not take the full pastoral responsibility. All tutors should have school-based in-service training to help them with their pastoral responsibility with bilingual pupils with little English.

Secondary schools should consider some special additional pastoral group sessions for pupils whose English is insufficient for them to benefit fully from normal monolingual tutor groups, led by a bilingual YPA, perhaps in the time of one normal monolingual tutor session a week.

Schools should consider starting informal discussion groups in lunch hours or after school, perhaps led by such a YPA, for those pupils with very little English and also possibly pupils of the same language who have learned rather more English to enable them to respond to any issues special to their group.

It is vital that LEAs (and perhaps the National Association for Pastoral Care in Education) should recognise that the pastoral care issues of bilingual education have hardly been touched upon in the research or literature, and that there are still problems to be resolved. It certainly would be valuable to see an action research study in Pastoral Care for bilingual pupils.

5.8 Overall languages policy

Many schools are familiar with attempts to develop a multicultural curriculum in which the ethnocentricity of the previous curriculum and learning materials is challenged and new perspectives introduced. In these efforts there has been a slower response to linguistic, as opposed to other cultural, diversity. Yet in many ways languages embody culture, and it is therefore impossible to be "multicultural without being "multilingual". New initiatives in the curriculum have often left the languages policy of a school untouched, with monolithic French a solid rock even in a would be multicultural curriculum. English departments still frequently operate as if they are teaching "English as a mother tongue", even where classrooms contain a sizeable proportion of bilingual pupils And in many schools, despite the potentially rich resource of linguistic diversity, there is no place in the curriculum for the study of language as a system, even though more than any other system, it unites human beings. The coherent bilingual education policy will give an important role to linguists. Their province is language as a system, together with para-, geo-, and socio-lingui and in a bilingual education policy teachers of languages will have a task beyond that of the traditional "French teacher". In most parts of the country multi-cultural education is seen, regrettably as an aspect of curriculum planning relevant only to schools with large proportion of children from ethnic minority families Similarly, the parochialism of the British view of languag diversity is anti-educational and compounds other prejudices. A Professor Eric Hawkins puts it:

> There is at present no place in the curriculum for discussing with pupils the phenomenon of language itself, as the distinguishing characteristic of the "articulate manner" or the relationship of English to other languages spoken in the U.K. and abroad. It is no accident that British society is marked by a high degree of linguistic parochialism. Linguistic tolerance does not come naturally, it has to be learned and to be worked at. The first reaction to language that cannot be understood ...

is suspicion, frustration, even anger. It is hard to believe that people who can behave so mysteriously (linguistically) can be like us at all.

(Hawkins, 1984, p.17)

His solution is a "language awareness" course for all, which surely appears to be an essential component of a true bilingual education policy.

The National Congress on Languages in Education has published a valuable series of descriptions of language awareness courses in UK schools. These descriptions make it clear that the total languages curriculum should be enriched by the world approach to languages. Where there has been discussion of bilingual education, it has been entirely in terms of the bilingual student and has ignored the valuable impact bilingual education could have on the curriculum of pupils whose mother tongue is English. Even the recent HMI survey on Mother-Tongue Teaching in School and Community hardly touches on this, mentioning only that "There were few instances of pupils other than mother-tongue speakers opting to take courses in the minority languages, even when, as in many cases, they were open to them" (HMI, 1984, pp 14-15). Indeed that report describes one school's languages curriculum which has a "world languages programme" for all pupils in the second year as if it were primarily for the speakers of minority languages, when actually it is one of the few examples of the existence of bilingual pupils affecting and improving the curriculum for pupils whose mother tongue is English (HMI, 1984, p.16).

Official documents on the place of languages in schools almost completely ignore the non-European languages. For the Schools Council Modern Languages Committee, before its demise, "second foreign languages" could mean only the European languages of German, Spanish, Italian, and Russian! It is an entirely Euro-centric document that treats "the second foreign language" as only related to "our political and economic development in Europe" (Schools Council Modern Languages Committee, 1982, p.13). The DES discussion document, Foreign Languages in the School Curriculum, devotes only some 22 lines to "Languages of Minority Communities", and merely notes that "among the questions to be considered are .... the scope for making ethnic community languages available as a curriculum option" (DES, 1983, p.11). Even writers urging the teaching of Asian languages in schools, often limit their exhortation to the teaching of these languages as mother tongues (e.g. Srivastava, 1982).

However, a few writers have urged the value to the whole curriculum for all of the linguistic minority speakers and their languages in the school. Harold Rosen and Tony Burgess declare:

In the process all pupils, speakers of all kinds, should be the beneficiaries, even though some of them were not being thought of when newly-arrived languages and dialects obliged us to take a closer look at the resources of all children and consider how those resources fare in the school system.   (Rosen and Burgess, 1980, p.140)

This book, <u>Languages and Dialects of London School Children</u>, celebrates linguistic diversity as a gain for all. In languages teaching it has been left to very few in education to urge that minority languages be available as "foreign" languages for all. One student teacher in a thesis has stressed the practical pedagogical value of teaching a language whose mother-tongue speakers are part of the society of our pupils:

> It seems ridiculous not to exploit the resources we have available. If the language being taught were Urdu, then it would be much easier for the pupils to experience the culture working. The Asian culture is there on the streets of most major cities in this country. It is there in the spoken form, used for everyday communication, and in its written form, on shop signs and newspapers. Apart from the contact with the culture being much easier, and much more equally shared, it would also mean that it could be more intense, and not just limited to a fortnight or three weeks.   (Pyle, 1980.)

So far in this discussion the two models have been discussed from the point of view of the student for whom English is not her or his first language. However, one of the great advantages of a fully developed bilingual education programme is the opportunities offered to native English speakers to gain from this programme. We are familiar from the French Lycee with English mother-tongue pupils choosing a bilingual education in French/English. In various parts of the world, families can choose Arabic, or Cantonese, or Bengali, for instance, as well as the European languages, as their bilingual second language and participate in the subject teaching and activities in and through that language.

The very existence in our schools of pupils who speak "the other languages of England" is potentially enriching for all pupils at all levels, e.g.:

(a) The language and cultures of the homes and heritage must assist the "humanities" teaching of people in society at all ages from infant school upwards.

(b) The knowledge and appreciation of literature in languages other than English must benefit all.

(c) The very existence in classes of bi- (or often tri-) lingual pupils, demonstrably equally proficient in, e.g. Arabic, English, and French, or seen to be moving from an equal control of Arabic and French to a new control of English, creates a new context for all language learning: in most UK schools learning a foreign language has felt strange, and the subject has been one of the most "distant" on the curriculum. In a school with bilingual students, with a properly developed languages curriculum, the pull to language success for all is very much more powerful.

(d) The existence of mother-tongue classes and bilingual education classes in minority and non-European languages is a boost to expanding the possibilities of a wider range of languages for all.

The languages of our minority-ethnic families must be made more visible in our schools. By recognising and valuing them, we can improve the confidence and self-esteem of speakers of these languages. We can also enhance the reputation of bilingual pupils in the eyes of their monolingual peers, who must be encouraged to discard prejudice against non-European languages and to appreciate the linguistic diversity of our society.

The following course of action is recommended:

(a) Languages-across-the curriculum policies should take into account the linguistic diversity of the school and the nature of that diversity and:

    (i) the positive role of the mother-tongue and second language support across the curriculum;

    (ii) that the learning development of all students will benefit from teaching methods which emphasise the positive uses of languages within mixed-ability groups;

    (iii) the need for adequate in-service training for all mainstream teachers dealing with bilingual students ("Every teacher has to be an E2L teacher").

(b) The languages curriculum of secondary schools should include some teaching of the community languages represented in the school and all pupils should have the opportunity of learning them (not just those who have them as a mother tongue). These languages should be represented in the option and examination provision and thus have the same status as other modern languages.

    (iv) The English syllabus should recognize the linguistic

diversity within the school, and English teachers should draw on literature and story-telling traditions of other languages and other cultures.

(v)   The remainder of the curriculum, especially humanities and arts, should incorporate an awareness and use of these languages.

(vi) A place should be found in the school curriculum for the study of language as a system.

The suggestions outlined above are as applicable to classrooms where the pupils are predominantly monolingual English speakers as they are to classrooms with large numbers of bilingual pupils. But an enormous advantage of teaching groups in which different languages are represented is the possibility of collaborative learning and of using the bilingual pupils as a resource. In the context of linguistic diversity, children can teach each other about language. Moreover a study of language "based on pupils' own knowledge and experience ... forges links between school and community which can only enhance the curriculum" (Rosen and Burgess, p.126). The linguistic proficiency of bilingual or even trilingual pupils should act as a powerful stimulus to language success among all pupils.

The outward manifestations of such a policy should not be confined to classrooms, so amongst other things:

(a)   Notices should include some in key languages, especially the more public ones in the school.

(b)   Nurseries, Educational Advice and Support Centres (proposed in 3.4), and local bookshops should include books on and in the languages of the schools and the literature in those languages.

(c)   More generally visitors, visits, public events and displays should include reference to and incorporate the school's community languages.

5.9 Conclusion

It is clear that "bilingual education" is built up from a number of components, and that the use of these will vary considerably. The overall aim is integration in which a variety of languages will be taught and used in a variety of combinations for their own sake and in the medium of "subject" teaching. All parts of the repertoire, from basic teaching in the mother tongue to bilingual teaching of subjects with E2L or mother-tongue teachers as partners to the subject teacher must be available for the schools to select from judiciously. The whole approach to what was previously called "foreign language" teaching will be changed, made more varied and enriched for all. For this to be possible, resource formulae are required for budgeting and deployment, and we will consider this in Chapter 7.

In brief, what is required in an overall concept of bilingual education, and for it to permeate the whole curriculum, especially the humanities, the arts, and the languages, it requires us all to:

(a) reassess the linguistic and cultural assumptions on which the curriculum is based: we are preparing all our students to live in a multiracial society which is also multilingual;

(b) make subject learning accessible to students who are learning through their second language: most teachers teach bilingual students;

(c) recognise students' bilingualism by providing for the use of both their first and second languages as subjects for study and tools for learning.

5   RECENT ARRIVALS

5.1 Introduction

In Chapter 5 we considered aspects of the teaching and learning of all bilingual learners, and, indeed, those who come to school with only English as their mother tongue. We must, however, not fall into the assumption of presuming that bilingual learners will have entered the British education system aged five and been educated in British schools continuously since. Most curriculum planning is, however, based on that assumption, and ignores the recently arrived pupil. A very special challenge lies with recently arrived bilingual pupils, who can be seriously disadvantaged by our system, the more so the older they are when they first join a British school and the less advanced the control of English that they bring with them.

Figures are not available for pupils who arrive in this country from education systems in which languages other than English are the teaching medium. However, we know that very many such students arrive at all ages of schooling. Again, these pupils vary from those with virtually no English (and in some cases illiterate in their own language) to pupils already equally proficient in two or more languages. Some come after very intensive and sophisticated education in various forms of national or international schools (often taught in a language medium other than their mother tongue), but others have had only a rudimentary or much fragmented schooling.

However able and well motivated they may be, bilingual learners who arrive after the start of formal schooling at 5 are at a particular disadvantage in our schools. Their educational progress is disrupted by the need to transfer their learning to a new language, and by the need to participate in a school system which expects them to achieve age-related goals, e.g. GCSE at 16 and A-levels at 18. In this respect even able students are at a disadvantage, and seldom obtain the qualifications which are commonly regarded by employers as the necessary starting point for jobs that have career prospects. Moreover, bilingual older arrivals may come from countries where the styles and range of jobs open to them are very different from what is available in Britain. So they are unlikely to have the skills or knowledge they need to look for work or further study or to deal with the institutional racism they are likely to meet.

The students in this age range fall into five categories:

(a)   those who have virtually no skills in either spoken or written English;

(b)   those who also have no literacy skills in their own language;

(c)   those with some previous experience in English, who, for example, may have learnt English as a foreign language in their home country;

(d)   those who have considerable English language skills, but need language support directly related to communication and study skills, together with "English for special purposes" in order to achieve their full career potential;

(e)   those who are already proficient bilinguals, often having had their previous education in the medium of English.

Often parents and sometimes teachers suggest that a young person should work with others of a younger age because of her or his current limitations in English. This goes against the grain of the UK education system, which is heavily "age-layered" compared with much of the rest of the developed world in which "grades" or "standards" are used rather than "years". It is very different from post-16 education, in which (e.g. at university) students of different ages work together. It is also severely discouraged by the fairly tight primary/secondary transfer procedures in most LEAs. Indeed, even our examination system, for all its new talk of "criteria referencing", symbolises age-layering in the phrase "sixteen-plus examination". As a result of these pressures, the huge majority of a "year" are likely to be of the same chronological age, and the later procedures of schooling, take-up in FE and grants, as well as dwindling self-regard, can work against the pupils who have been (as others see it) "put down a year".

Although all post-five arrivals thus face difficulties, the situation is especially acute for those who arrive of secondary age, and even more so for those over the age of fourteen, unless they are already "highly proficient" in English. In our provision for students between fourteen and eighteen it is quite clear that education is organised for young people who have had their school careers in England and so are inside the system. However able and well motivated they may be, bilingual learners who arrive after fourteen are therefore at a particular disadvantage. To avoid programmed underachievement for older recent arrivals, it is necessary to re-examine both statutory and non-statutory provision.

6.2 Secondary schools

The first three years of secondary schools all follow a pattern of compulsory subjects for both girls and boys encompassing most aspects of learning. Entry directly into these subjects, often soon after arriving and having had a change of home, adult guardians, town, school, and languages sometimes presents the pupil with a number of severe difficulties:

(a) a lack of the background, presumed by the syllabus, learning material, and teacher. For example, secondary science is built on a foundation of concepts (such as classification) and skills (such as measurement) normally developed in primary schools in the UK, but which some pupils will not necessarily have gained in a compatible way elsewhere;

(b) the inability to understand simple instructions by monolingual teachers;

(c) some confusion about the expectations, procedures, and personnel of a school.

Newly-arrived pupils with little English should be immediately taken on roll and welcomed into the school and a Tutor Group, but should have the benefit of a planned induction, both pastoral and in the main curriculum. The length and mode of this induction will vary, and a number of different components from the matrix in Chapter 5 can be combined. Whilst the pupil should be helped to feel part of the Tutor Group or Form and the school, sudden and total immersion into the complete range of activities should be avoided.

As described earlier, in the older years, secondary education poses even greater problems for many recently arrived students. In these years most subjects are generally taught according to exam syllabi. All students are required to take certain compulsory subjects, but others they can choose (or be rejected by!). In the fourth and fifth years the course is in effect a five-term one, with the teaching planned to cover the examination syllabus from the start of the fourth year to the end of the spring terms of the fifth. Entry after the start of the course is difficult in terms of syllabus, and in the fifth year nearly impossible. The course-work emphasis of GCSE has exacerbated this problem.

E2L support for secondary-school students of these older ages is rare, and students in schools with no E2L support are often obliged to lose up to 50% of their subject-learning time in order to get language support off-site. For late arrivals in these schools, there is virtually no chance to gain public qualifications at a time when they would be useful. Further, the level of support available in most schools which do have E2L teachers enables most of them only to offer support outside the subject classroom, e.g. withdrawal groups or alternative E2L options. This isolation presents a number of problems:

(a) What subjects is E2L to be set against?

(b) What is the content of E2L support to be?

(c) What marketable qualifications can be adopted to validate study in E2L groups?

Thus, to sum up, entry into "the option years" can present a number of problems:

(a) Bilingual students are sometimes denied access to certain subjects at a suitable level because they do not have sufficient English to sit for public exams in those subjects.

(b) Different criteria are used for placing bilingual children:

(i)   Language development is taken as the criteria for acceptance into the options rather than academic knowledge or potential.

(ii) They may have to work in a year below their chronological age if it is considered they do not have sufficient English to learn a subject through the medium of English. Thus they may find themselves taking first-level qualifications 2/3 years later than their English mother-tongue peers are, or they may reach nineteen with no qualifications and face the prospect of having to meet fees for courses in FE.

(c) Students are restricted in their choice of subjects because:

(i)   Some option groups may be "full". Having been arranged at the end of the 3rd year, they will be staffed to take a finite number of students and new entrants are difficult to fit in;

(ii) Entry to a subject is a two-way negotiation: if staff do not feel the student has a reasonable chance of success they are not likely to welcome her or him to the group.

(d) The above facts are the more serious as alternatives to exam options are often "fringe", e.g. "remedial support" in which there is no recognised syllabus or certification.

(e) Lack of suitable courses in schools particularly discriminates against girls who wish to continue studying in single-sex provision and therefore cannot take up FE courses.

(f) There are no schools which are able to offer adequate E2L support for 4th, 5th, and 6th years across the curriculum.

Very similar problems arise in school sixth forms, and there is thus a tendency to encourage recently arrived bilingual students to apply to a Further Education College rather than a school, even if other educational arguments would suggest otherwise.

6.3   From school to work

The introduction of bilingual older-arrival pupils to job opportunities requires co-operation on the part of bilingual teachers, careers teachers, officers of the Careers Service (such as detached employment officers and outreach workers) and mother-tongue speakers (e.g. ethnic minority community workers in the neighbourhood). Mother-tongue speakers have a vital role to play in explaining job opportunities to bilingual pupils and their parents and in giving individual encouragement and counselling.

The Careers Service also has an important role in providing a link between bilingual pupils and training opportunities. A commendable practice has been followed in North London of establishing contact with pupils during their third year, maintaining it during the fourth year, and interviewing each pupil at length early in the fifth year. It is important that officers of the Service keep in touch with representatives of minority communities. This, of course, can only happen if and when bilingual pupils can be encouraged and enabled to apply for entry to the Careers Service.

6.4   Further education

The structural division between statutory school and the non-statutory provision for post-16-year-olds has an effect on students' progress quite unlike other major divisions. Selective provision replaces provision by need, even though individual institutions attempt to ameliorate it through the courses they offer. This change of motive is at the root of many of the problems faced by bilingual students. Our society has decided on a set of age-related boundaries (for statutory education, for the first stages of training, and for Further Education). Those who have not spent the "normal" time, and those who are still acquiring the necessary fluency in English, cannot easily fit this pattern.

They will reach their eighteenth birthday all too soon. After that a very large number of possibilities are beyond their reach. Getting the best use of this period, value for time, has to be the keynote of provision and planning for each of these students.

Post-sixteen provision can discriminate against bilingual students on four grounds: requirements for fluency in English, requirements concerning general education, proof of residence qualifications, and entry tests.

(a) Fluency: This is largely an issue of insufficient language support for courses and can be remedied by supplying that support. Any requirement for fluency prior to admission results in students attempting to enter courses when they are too old to gain credit for them and being subsequently prevented from progressing to further levels.

(b) General education: Discrimination here operates in two ways:-

(i) Some courses require a specified level of general educational achievement. Although many students come from overseas with formal qualifications these are usually disregarded by the British education system.

(ii) Many bilingual students will have had their general education disrupted by the need to transfer their learning into English. There are too few general education courses which cater for this group as opposed to "remedial" English mother-tongue learners.

(c) Residence: Entrance to non-statutory provision may confuse a student's immigration status if she or he is a recent arrival. The regulations for admission to colleges as a "home" student demand that bilingual students prove their entitlement. The DES's "ordinary residence" requirement further restricts certain residents to Sixth Form provision even when it is unsuitable. Conversely, many students who are not able to claim to be "ordinary residents" paradoxically have to choose Further Education (or a fee-paying school) as FE has to charge fees. Any system based on the current FE regulations will perpetuate and extend this institutionally racist device. Teachers and counsellors working with recent arrivals need to be aware of the general implications of immigration law and the Nationality Act in order to alert students and support them in seeking detailed, informed advice. Actual advice is best given by people with relevant legal experience, able to communicate with the students and their families.

(d) Entry tests: Many of the standard assessment tests have an actual though not explicit cultural language bias that effectively acts as discrimination against bilingual applicants on grounds that have nothing to do with the suitability of the course for the student.

Once in a college, provision of E2L support is enormously variable according to which college the young person applies. Three features are common, however:

(a) A young person who has to do a preliminary year of E2L only in order to gain access to a course may be faced with problems over fees because of the time it takes.

(b) There is very little consultation and negotiation with the community as to what courses are needed.

(c) All provision is co-educational; some families may be hesitant to send girls to college because of this.

The system argues that facilities be provided according to the numbers of students enrolling. If students are deterred from enrolling, the system feels justified in limiting E2L and mother-tongue resources and this has the continued effect of depressing enrolment. Put simply, there is a cyclical mechanism for excluding students which must be broken.

6.5. **Conclusion**

The older a bilingual learner is when he or she enters British education the greater the mis-match between the needs of the bilingual learner and our educational provision, unless he or she is already very proficient in English. Particularly between the ages of fourteen and eighteen our education presents itself as a "completion", dependent on earlier stages. "Fresh starts" are rare and difficult, and most qualifications have age and time criteria.

Yet older arrivals frequently need more time to reach their objectives than the conventional cut-off points allow. At sixteen their access to continued education or to training may be restricted by the system's attitude to their level of fluency in English, particularly their literacy, and to their general education. Indeed, for many older arrivals there is a conflict between our demands and their expectations. They may have come from an education system that does not confine opportunities to prescribed ages. Some expect to continue studying until they reach advanced qualifications - for however long this may take. They may even be unaware of our cut-off points.

Especial thought and provision should be given to older arrivals. The following suggestons are put forward as a starting point:

School

(a) An authority should ensure that recently arrived bilingual pupils are placed appropriately in schools. Experience has shown that schools with falling rolls accept pupils but cannot always provide enough E2L support, while schools with full rolls need not accept pupils even if they have E2L provision. Authorities should monitor the number of new arrivals each term, and plan E2L provision according to the needs revealed by statistical evidence.

(b) Bilingual older-arrivals should be given access to the full range of the curriculum. We are concerned that some schools seem to offer them only so-called "practical" subjects.

(c) Bilingual older-arrivals need continuing language support. Without it, the great majority of them at present leave school with a low grade in English, although they may achieve a high one in subjects such as Art, Woodwork, and Mathematics, where success is less dependent on mastery of language. But without English language skills, they cannot compete on equal terms in the job market.

(d) Bilingual older-arrivals should not be excluded from entering the Sixth Form. They and their parents need to be better informed about the options (Sixth Form, Further Education, and others) open to them after the fifth year.

(e) Wherever possible, access to education should be available in mother-tongue languages. It should be possible for some subjects, for example Mathematics, to be taught in mother tongues.

From School to Work

(f) Wherever there are known to be bilingual older-arrival pupils a meeting should be convened - on the initiative, perhaps, of a school, or of the Careers Service, or of the Bilingual

Education Centre - of the teachers, Careers Service officers, community workers and any others who can be held to identify the needs of this particular target group of pupils, with a view to strengthening communication and co-operation.

Further Education

(g) For those students who have virtually no skills in written or spoken English we recommend more courses, beginning no later than March of their school-leaving year, which emphasise communication and literacy skills and take "the world of work" as the vehicle for language learning. Courses of this kind might take place in each school that has pupils needing it; or pupils from several schools could be brought together in the Bilingual Education Centre; or courses could be run as a "multilink arrangement" in F.E. A pupil would spend part of her or his time in school and a number of days each week at the college, thus establishing a link which would prevent her or his becoming "lost" during the summer holiday at the end of the fifth year, and which would familiarise her or him during the last weeks of school with the opportunities which further education has to offer. Moreover, we believe there is no reason why further education colleges should not provide courses of this type for young people who have passed the statutory school-leaving age. Such a course in a college could best be provided by specialist E2L staff in a general education department and be set in the context of a variety of courses, vocational and otherwise, which can give sympathetic support to the basic language work.

(h) For those students with moderate ability in spoken and written English we recommend an induction course of the type pioneered in Camden's Operation Springboard project. Such a course would require close co-operation on the part of the Manpower Services Commission and an FE college of the kind which has made the Camden project possible, together with the help of the Careers Service.

(i) The role of the Careers Service in identifying pupils has already been suggested above, but FE colleges have an equally important part to play; we would want to see much closer liaison on a regular basis between specialist staff in colleges who are concerned with E2L and teachers in schools in the interests of identifying, at an early stage, those E2L recent arrivals whose needs can best be met by the induction course, and the implementation of a coherent bilingual education policy.

(j) For students who have considerable language skills and obvious career potential we suggest:

(i)   some of these could go straight into an FE college,
      provided there were suitably flexible and diverse
      provision, including appropriate vocational or subject
      examination courses with specialist language support. If
      pupils in this category are to go straight from school
      into colleges, many colleges will wish to be more flexible
      in the options that they offer; at present their E2L
      resources and thus provision are often inadequate;

(ii) other pupils in this third category might go straight into
      the induction course and then into a work-placement, with
      the object of discovering during the training experience
      whether they wanted to go into a job or whether they
      wanted to go into an FE or other course to seek
      qualifications.

(h)   The automatic imposition of fees in FE Colleges at the age of
      nineteen should be examined to explore the possibility of
      removing or varying it for those entering the British system of
      education late.

7   RESOURCING AND SUPPORT

7.1   A Coherent Approach to Bilingual Education

If a policy for bilingual education is to work successfully, it is
essential that the current human and material resources relating to
all aspects of multi-ethnic education and bilingual education are
reviewed, rationalised, and, in places, enhanced.

LEAs' resources covering the whole field of multi-ethnic education
have been developed in a disparate way over a number of years in
response to discernible needs within the schools and the communities
they serve. While the professionals working within this area of
concern have contributed greatly towards improving the quality of
educational provision, there remains a lack of continuity, coordination, and coherence within the service as a whole. It is now
essential to take stock of the current overall provision for
bilingual education, which does not fit conveniently into the old
structures.

A critical appraisal of the present system follows, to identify its
strengths and weaknesses, as a first step towards developing a
coherent and coordinated approach to the future allocation of
resources.

7.2 Administrative structures

The current human and material resources of many authorities are divided generally between schools, Adult Education, and Further Education (FE). This historical division of responsibilities hinders a a "whole-family" approach. The structure of the inspectorate in most LEAs tends to be likewise divided into separate areas of responsibility. Thus, only informal links exist between the schools, AES, and FE, and these have been forged on the anvil of goodwill at a local level in recognition of the need for greater cohesiveness and coordination within the service as a whole.

The establishment of co-ordinated Tertiary Education planning, when viewed in the above context, must be to the advantage of bilingual learners. For the first time within the ILEA, for instance, secondary schools' sixth forms and colleges of FE will be resourced jointly, with the Divisional Education Officer responsible (in collaboration with the Inspectorate and colleagues in schools and colleges) for the identification of educational need and the allocation of resources across the 16-19 age group. Closer links will therefore be forged between schools and colleges and the development of courses especially designed for the bilingual student will be made that much easier. Increased continuity in the learning process could result from tertiary arrangements and will certainly ease the plight of the older bilingual student.

7.3 A Centre for Bilingual Education

Where they are present, Language Centres in the LEAs date in concept from a period of low numbers of pupils requiring E2L and when most of the tuition was provided to pupils at the Centre for five half-days a week.

As is clear from this paper many parts of the country are now facing new demands that have no present source of supply. The new demands come from:

(a) the substantially increased numbers of bilingual pupils,

(b) increased diversity,

(c) a demand for a coherent bilingual policy,

(d) a need to train teachers for E2L and mother-tongue teaching and to work with bilingual pupils in the normal classroom,

(e) the addition of mother-tongue languages,

(f) the need to coordinate the supply of teachers.

A centre for Bilingual Education as a central, co-ordinating resource base is a possible solution we have mentioned from time to time in this paper.

While we hope that most bilingual education will be on-site in schools, the responsibilities of a local authority or divisional Centre for Bilingual Education might include :

(a) providing the focal point for all discussion, research, school support and development of practice, and sharing of resources, for bilingual education in the authority,

(b) working in consultation with schools on such matters as the accuracy and completeness of a language census,

(c) working with the Education Office on forecasting school bilingual populations,

(d) acting as a Teachers' Centre for all E2L and mother-tongue teachers,

(e) organising supply teachers for bilingual education,

(f) organising posts for bilingual education to work in schools on secondment for a short or long period as is required,

(g) providing the base for aides and translators,

(h) acting as the base for small mother-tongue classes,

(i) continuing to offer E2L classes as required,

(j) co-ordinating with schools to offer some bilingual subject teaching to pupils from schools who have insufficient numbers to manage it themselves,

(k) as a reprographic centre offering also a translating service to schools, and other organisations and groups with an interest in education,

(l) working closely with community classes, and the proposed Educational Advice and Support Centres (see 3.4), in all appropriate ways.

(m) distribution of information from outside agencies, such as public libraries, health centres, G.P.'s, Social Services housing departments, homeless persons units, youth clubs, under 5's facilities, community centres, community relations councils and supplementary schools.

7.4 Forecasting

A procedure which is as accurate as possible is required to forecast the arrival of pupils in any area and the transfer of pupils from primary to secondary school, so that adequate resources can be available in the appropriate schools ready for the education of those pupils.

In areas of high mobility and current immigration, forecasting machinery is unable to provide detailed statistics on significant shifts of the population or provide information on the movement of individual families and their children within or into the an authority. This is a wide inner-city problem. It will remain very difficult to predict sudden movement resulting, for instance, from changes in housing policies or external political events. Nevertheless, a much improved information flow should be possible and would benefit many aspects of education provision, especially resource provision. In ILEA, for example, a co-ordinator could establish a close working relationship with London Boroughs, foreign embassies, and the Home and Foreign Offices to ensure that any population movements will in future be carefully monitored. Information and detailed statistics relating to movements of individual families and general population trends could then be forwarded on a regular basis. Because housing patterns dictate shifts in population, ideally the co-ordinator would have to liaise very closely with housing departments. The details of this are beyond the scope of this paper, but it is vital that others should take this responsibility.

7.5 Needs-based resourcing

In order that resource requirements can be forecast, it is essential to devise needs-based formulae that are easy to apply. Needs-based resourcing should be seen as separate from and in addition to roll-based resourcing. In ILEA at present 40% of the pupils in some schools are bilingual pupils, while other schools may only have 2% on roll. If schools have to employ this roll-based money to cover their bilingual needs, the authority is in effect favouring the non-bilingual pupils in the latter category of schools. This leads to great resentment and is surely a clear form of institutional racism*.

---

* 'institutional racism': I use this phrase in what I take to be the objective agreed sense: procedures or sets of rules that, whatever their intention, work differentially for people of different racial backgrounds, and thus inadvertently discriminate against certain racial groups. It is important to remember that very often these procedures do not have this intention. Lack of knowledge, thought, or sensitivity in the devising has allowed them to so discriminate.

M.M.

Once the resource requirements have been forecast, it is equally essential that they are met: i.e. that they can be applied for and authorised readily, without a school having to resort to pressurising and appeals. If "equality" and "anti-racism" are to have meaning as reality, the resources agreed as appropriate should be obtained by the schools as of right - like any other aspects of resourcing. Indeed a form of institutional racism can be implied if resources for bilingual education have to be cajoled by protracted bargaining.

This means in effect that:

(a) a census should be carried out as frequently as possible, and supplemented by forecasting as far as it can intelligently be done;

(b) schools should have a clear machinery that they can use to adjust the actuality with the forecast;

(c) resources should be quickly and flexibly available to correspond with changing needs.

There should clearly be contininuous monitoring of the use of resources for bilingual education.

There is considerable confusion about the term "Special Needs" being used to embrace both bilingual education provision relating to educational priority areas and physical, emotional, and learning needs. A separation of these different needs as identified by an LEA is of importance.

Formulae are required for all aspects of bilingual education, which can be conveniently divided into: E2L teachers, mother-tongue teachers, aides, and translators.

7.6 E2L teachers

Different LEAs use diferent methods of establishing authorised staff. In the ILEA, currently E2L posts are allocated in schools following an annual review of needs. Resource allocation is based on the whole on language competence levels of pupils and those are incorporated into a set formula which in turn determines the points scored and hence the number of teaching posts which each school is entitled to. One needs-based approach, including the formula, is as follows:

Beginners: number of pupils, multiplied by 6
Second stage: number of pupils, multiplied by 3
Third stage: number of pupils, multiplied by 1.

The points scored attracts a notional staffing allocation for bilingual education, for example, for primary schools 45 = .3 of a teacher, 220 points = 1 teacher.

In the past, E2L teacher entitlement has been based strictly according to the scores obtained by the above process. This can make teaching in schools with low scores impossible. The latest weightings, however, allow more room for manoeuvre and are weighted slightly in favour of low-scoring schools. The pupil number and level score need to be adjusted according to the scope of a school.

Serious problems of resourcing schools remain, however, despite the above needs-based approach. Estimates of needs can be based on figures two years out of date. Bilingual education supply cover is not available; some schools' bilingual education teams are too small to provide professional support for colleagues or sufficient incentive payments to attract teachers of high calibre and experience in bilingual education leadership. It is essential therefore that we must attempt first to provide:

(a) a more accurate and up-to-date assessment of bilingual education needs;

(b) a pool of resources which would be made available when sudden influxes of bilingual pupils occur.

There is also the need to recognise that schools have to accept bilingual pupils but some do not have the staffing expertise to offer the appropriate facilities. An authority should therefore ensure that there is a teacher in each school with a responsibility post for bilingual education.

The official categories used by many LEAs for bilingual pupils are based on their command of spoken English and this does not allow for the extra tuition required by pupils who may speak English quite well, but still cannot read or write in the language. Thus, pupils categorised as Stage 2 or even 3 according to their abilites in the spoken language may still be at Stage 1 in the development of their literacy skills.

If we refer back to the weighting of pupils referred to earlier we will see that Stage Three pupils attract the lowest weighting. This must create under-achievement in pupils and is a form of, as the Hargreaves Report describes it, "subtle deprivation" (Committee of Enquiry into the Curriculum and Organisation of Secondary Schools, 1984, para. 3.7.7., p.46). It is right that a priority should be given to children with no English, but what happens to those stage 2 and 3 pupils who are withdrawn less and less for specific language learning? At present resources are not adequate to give support to bilingual education above the basic education. Once they cease to be beginners, bilingual pupils spend most of their school time with main-stream teachers, but the present resourcing takes no account of the collaborative staffing required to help those pupils continue their education bilingually. There is therefore a need to recognise further differential stages within the three categories referred to earlier. A systematic approach must be developed to what is a complex problem, a system which does not ignore the cultural or linguistic backgrounds of the pupils or their previous educational experiences.

7.7. Mother-tongue or Community-language Teachers

There is a crucial contribution to bilingual education to be made by teachers who are themselves bilingual, and both teach a mother tongue (community language or heritage language) and teach through it.

Most authorities currently appear to have no staffing formula for such teachers. This contrasts badly with the arrangements in, for example, Massachusetts, USA, where formulae have statutory power, or Toronto, Canada, where any group of 25 speakers of a language automatically attracts authorisation for a teacher who is bilingual in that language. A formula must be devised by each LEA for mother-tongue teachers.

There is then the problem of availability. A LEA must attract teachers who are fluent in the main minority languages spoken within its boundaries. The authority needs to look at its criteria for their qualification and the recognition of experienced mother-tongue and other teachers. The problem facing the teachers who qualify in some other countries is that the DES will not always recognise their qualifications. Local authorities are also in somewhat of a cleft stick because they cannot therefore employ them as teachers, yet unless they are in employment they cannot be seconded to courses where they will gain the recognised qualification to teach. Authorities should therefore consider advertising in the relevant press and employing overseas-trained teachers as instructors, and then second them to courses where they would be able to obtain recognised teaching qualifications.

New appointment procedures for teachers and new courses must of course be developed in close co-operation with initial teacher-training establishments to ensure that the country can obtain a supply of highly qualified teachers fluent in the main minority languages.

7.8 Bilingual aides

The mixture of teaching modes offered in section 5 implies occasions when the main medium of instruction would be English, but help would be required by adult speakers of the pupils' mother tongue to explain, interpret, and facilitate. Many primary schools are already using such "helpers" to good educational effect.

It is impressive to note the arrangements made in Australia, the USA, and Canada to introduce such aides into schools (see Appendix B). British schools are used to the notion of "aides" in primary schools, but the Australian model refers to paid professional assistants from the community who offer in-class support to bilingual learners. We envisage there being three categories of adults interested in such work:

(a) those who have teaching qualifications in their country of origin, but are as yet not recognised by DES;

(b) those who would like to acquire teacher-training;

(c) young "new generation" adults who have successfully come through the education system and are interested in helping younger members of their community.

This is not a proposal for schools to avoid a true bilingual education programme. Rather the hope is that "aides" would be useful both as classroom assistants and as bridges with the community served by the school. For such posts to be given due recognition and pay, their job description should be drawn up by the LEAs, and the relevant communities involved in the appointments.

7.9 Supply teachers

Hitherto there have been few supply teachers for either the limited amount of mother-tongue work that has been achieved nor for the much larger amount of E2L teaching. This has meant, for instance, that some primary schools have been without any E2L teaching for more than a term as illness has hit the one teacher. It has also often meant that pupils normally withdrawn from a class in both secondary and primary schools for specific E2L teaching have been "returned" unexpectedly on certain days because of the illness of the normal bilingual education teacher. It seems completely unfair that this should be so. It is therefore necessary to advertise for and possibly train supply teachers in bilingual education, both E2L and mother-tongue. Such teachers should not normally be part of the main supply pool, but should be on "permanent cover" contracts.

7.10 Translators

The philosophy and policies we have described in previous sections require the services of translators on a number of occasions in certain (but by no means all) of the relevant languages. A needs-based formula would need to be devised to produce a staffing establishment.

The translators would work from a Centre for Bilingual Education, and schools, colleges, the Education Office, and community groups would be able to book them by arrangement.

7.11 Responsibility posts

With the traditional in-school responsibility for much curriculum planning, team leadership, career development, monitoring, and assessment, all teams of teachers in a school must have an adequate "structure" of scale posts to take responsibility for leadership and management. However, there is a paradox in the staffing of teachers for bilingual education. Whereas it is common for teachers for bilingual education (mother-tongue and E2L specialists, or combinations of these) to be authorised on a needs-based formula and seconded to schools so that there can be flexibility as population requirements make necessary, above-scale-one posts are strictly on a roll-based formula. This means that the size of a bilingual education team can grow very fast in a school, which, on the one hand, can not redeploy its responsibility points to this aspect of staffing, nor, on the other hand, can appeal for additional points (unless it is below its maximum). Obviously, however the restructuring of the system is to take place, it is important that the bilingual team in a school should be well led, well organised, and have career prospects. It is also important for the service as a whole that there should be proper career prospects for bilingual education teaching. This principle will continue to need stressing under whatever structural arrangements follow Burnham. We suggest that the most appropriate solution in present Burnham conditions is that a certain number of Burnham points be attached to a Bilingual Education Centre, and that teachers appointed to these should then be "seconded" with their responsibility points to the school. There are inevitable problems with this proposal. One is the fact that such a pool is dependent on schools being able to use these staff. Another is the fact that there are then no in-school appointments. However, this system would replicate in the school's points structure the needs-based formula for bilingual education teachers, and would allow the bilingual team (however internally organised) to have an appropriate responsibility structure without the need to distort the other structure of the school. In schools with a large proportion of bilingual pupils, especially with a large proportion in the early stages, the needs-related staffing will require needs-related reponsibility posts for proper leadership and management.

7.12 In-service Implications

Implementing an effective policy of bilingual education will have far-reaching implications for in-service training programmes provided by an authority for its teachers. In schools where E2L departments have either been small or non-existent, newly appointed teachers need a massive commitment of time on the part of other teachers and the appropriate physical and material resources in order to become totally effective. It is imperative, therefore, that such schools are cognisant of these facts and thus prepared to establish induction programmes for the incoming teachers and for the existing staff of the school. These programmes should be established with the support of the Inspectorate and the staff of the Centre for Bilingual Education. The following types of training will be required.

ALL TEACHERS

(a) Anti-racism: To explain how a monolingual education system which devalues the languages and bilingualism of its pupils is perpetuating a form of institutionalized racism.

(b) Language diversity: To inform teachers about the languages, cultures, and educational background of their bilingual pupils.

(c) Community languages: To encourage some teachers to learn one of the languages represented in their local community. (This could perhaps be arranged by enabling teachers to attend classes set up for pupils with their own school.)

BILINGUAL TEACHERS

To develop the ability in some subject or mother-tongue teachers to teach bilingually to certain stages, e.g. the early years in humanities, sciences, and maths, and the later years in literature, commercial studies, and humanities.

MOTHER-TONGUE TEACHERS

(a) to provide teachers of community languages with a qualification recognized by the DES, so that they can be appointed to schools on normal professional terms;

(b) to ensure that mother-tongue teachers are equipped to teach basic literacy in their languages and to organize mixed-level classes.

E2L TEACHERS

In particular training is urgently needed:

(a)   to develop skills for the teaching of basic literacy;

(b)   to enable E2L teachers to work more effectively in
      collaboration with subject and class teachers.

MAINSTREAM TEACHERS

Since in many schools all mainstream teachers have to teach
bilingual children, they all have to be, in one sense, bilingual/E2L
teachers.   But it is unrealistic to expect this unless a thorough
programme of in-service training is organised.   The broad aims of
such a programme would be:

(a)   to encourage positive attitudes to community languages and
      bilingualism, and to develop strategies for utilizing the
      bilingual resources of the school;

(b)   to increase understanding of the role of language in learning,
      in particular the importance of talk in developing E2L pupils'
      language skills and all pupils' learning;

(c)   to introduce subject teachers to E2L techniques and methods of
      ensuring that lessons and materials are more accessible to
      pupils with limited proficiency in English.

LANGUAGE TEACHERS

If pupils who come to secondary school as English mother-tongue
monolinguals are to benefit linguistically from the presence of such
a variety of bilingual pupils in the school, "language awareness" or
"world languages" courses will be taken up by many schools. This is
going to require specific training in non-European languages for
most language teachers.

7.13 The Inspectorate

A policy for bilingual education, therefore, must ensure that a
formal working framework is established within an LEA to bring the
disparate parts of the inspectorate and administration together in
order for them to monitor the development of policy in a systematic
way and to relate resourcing truly to curriculum needs.   A fully
augmented bilingual programme will need especial leadership and
require the equivalent of a full-time inspector to co-ordinate E2L
and mother-tongue teaching, both in schools, in Centres for
Bilingual Education, and in community classes and summer projects.

7.14 Learning resources

There is a need to develop resources, especially for the production of more mother-tongue support material of quality. For some work in particular there is no published material, and teachers in schools are working long hours preparing their own.

E2L teachers could benefit from a co-ordinated programme for developing E2L materials especially for beginners and literacy pupils. At present individual teachers or E2L departments make their own materials and there is a wasteful reduplication of effort. An E2L curriculum project like Ilpac or Smile would not only reduce the unreasonable workload of E2L teams, but also produce better quality materials. (Both are highly successful examples of the ILEA facilitating the work of teachers and inspectors to develop for themselves curriculum and related materials for needs not otherwise met. Smile is a widely used Maths scheme that must be one of the most successful examples of curriculum development in the country.)

7.15 Accommodation

Bilingual education has accommodation implications which, not surprisingly, have not been worked out in standard schedules of accommodation. Although much of the work fits into standard accommodation, there is a considerable need for additional small rooms for groups who are on occasions withdrawn for small-group mother-tongue or E2L tuition.

In schools with falling rolls, or newly defined lower forms of entry than originally planned, there is not usually too much difficulty finding the space. However, it is always difficult in full schools, and, in any school, it can be difficult to negotiate the new use of space released by falling rolls. The teaching-space implications of the bilingual education patterns should be studied.

7.16 Conclusion

Although resources are tightly controlled and expansion difficult, it is clear that the needs of bilingual education have been less well looked after in the UK than in other countries, and that a major reconsideration of forecasting, budgeting, deploying, organising, and monitoring resources is absolutely essential.

A national Standing Committee on Bilingual Education would best monitor the implementation of a Policy on Bilingual Education and provide a focus for the views and wishes of the minority-language communities whose education we serve.

Curriculum Models

The typology used by Fishman (1976), consisting of four basic stages
within a bilingual programme of development, is a helpful analysis.
He describes:

(a) Transitional bilingualism

(b) Monoliterate bilingualism

(c) Biliterate bilingualism (partial)

(d) Biliterate bilingualism (full)

**Suggested continuum indicating stages of progression leading
to the establishment of a Fully Bilingual Policy for Schools:**

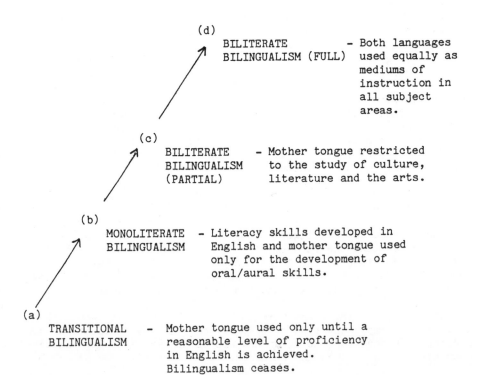

(d)

BILITERATE   – Both languages
BILINGUALISM (FULL)   used equally as
                          mediums of
                          instruction in
                          all subject
                          areas.

(c)

BILITERATE   – Mother tongue restricted
BILINGUALISM   to the study of culture,
(PARTIAL)   literature and the arts.

(b)

MONOLITERATE   – Literacy skills developed in
BILINGUALISM   English and mother tongue used
                          only for the development of
                          oral/aural skills.

(a)

TRANSITIONAL   – Mother tongue used only until a
BILINGUALISM   reasonable level of proficiency
                          in English is achieved.
                          Bilingualism ceases.

(a) Transitional Bilingualism is defined by Wright in the following way:

> These are programmes where the child's first language is used in the early school grades along with the language which is the main medium of instruction, but only up until the point in time when skill in the medium of instruction enables it to be used alone.   (Wright, 1982, p.7)

This model is compensatory in nature.   It implies that there is something lacking in the family and the child.   The children are looked upon as "deficit systems" (Bernstein in Wright, 1982, p.8).

The use of mother tongue seems to help children in the early stages of education, but the institution is using the language solely as a bridge for the introduction of the language of instruction. The aim is, in fact, to replace the mother tongue by that of the majority language.   Once the mother tongue is dropped, immersion in the majority language brings with it a denial of the child's cultural heritage and identity.   This can alienate the child from both the institution and the family.

The effects in linguistic terms are negative or "subtractive".   The child's development within the majority language will be limited by the lack of concepts that would normally be acquired in the mother tongue.   Instead of the institution building on the child's language, it forces the child to disregard his or her roots, and so stunts potential growth.

Institutions adopting the approach appear to reach out to the community.   In fact they are making a value-judgement on these languages, implying that the needs of education - and the needs of pupils - can only be implemented through the majority language. The child must fit into the institution.

The message to bilingual pupils and the community is that any adjustment must come from them rather than from the institution. The message to the monolingual child is first there need be no adjustment on their part, and secondly that the bilingual community and their languages are inferior.

(b) Monoliterate Bilingualism

This model encourages the development of oral/aural skills in both the language of the homes and the medium of instruction, but literacy skills are developed only in the language which is the medium of instruction.

In contrast to the transitional programmes, monoliterate bilingualism maintains the mother tongue and culture of pupils throughout schooling thus ensuring confidence and self-esteem and an acceptance of the institution. The effects of this is that the minority pupils benefit from schooling and are more sympathetic to the majority culture and language within the institution and outside it.

Whilst there are undeniable gains in interpersonal communication, the fact that literacy is not developed in the mother tongue in such a model seems to gloss over the powerful influence of the printed word as perceived by the community and linguistically falls short of the enriching development that reading and writing bring to linguistic and cognitive development at least up to a level which goes beyond mere oral competence such as the use of the mother tongue for academic purposes.

(c) Biliterate Bilingualism (Partial)

In this kind of programme, the goal is literacy in both the medium of interaction and the home language. But mother-tongue skills are restricted to use in schools to studying particular subject matter usually the literature and arts of the culture associated with the mother tongue. The main medium of instruction is the language through which literacy is exercised in the technological, science, and economic subjects. (Wright, 1982, p.7).

Like monoliterate bilingualism, this approach works positively for the children in that their culture heritage and identify are both approved and enhanced. They can be proud of their roots and benefit more successfully from institutions and society, however dominated these are by the majority language.

Every child should have the right to full development of his/her existing skills and educational potential. The mother tongue is an essential component of his/her identity and culture. This provision would help children maintain a consistent picture of themselves and their family and would decrease the gulf between home and school ... . (NCMTT in Wright, 1982, p.12)

The opportunity to further their literacy skills in their own language ensures that children advance linguistically. However, to equate mother-tongue instruction only with culture-related subjects is to deny children the right to grow to a full intellectual capacity. It certainly gives them a good grounding to go beyond the provision in schools and to make their own informed choices. It gives them control of their own language. But it does not give them full access to education as the monolingual child fluent in the majority language experiences it.

(d) Biliterate Bilingualism (Full)

In this type of programme, all students develop skills in both languages and both languages are used equally as mechanisms of instruction in all subject areas.

Only this model seems to imply that no distinction is made between monolingual and bilingual students. But the contexts of such programmes are rare and would take the form of immersion in the old language in certain content areas or might be prevalent more frequently among bilingual elites, where enrichment rather than compensation is the target.

The extent to which such programmes are successful has been related to criteria such as the percentage of take-up of such courses, the attitudes of pupils to the languages, but more crucially, to the amount of support within the community. According to an International Study of Secondary Bilingual Education:

... Not only is community consensus needed if bilingual education is to succeed, but ... the help of the major language group is needed as much as, if not more than, the help of the minority language groups ... . The main trouble with foreign language learning thus far has been that it was an entirely school dependent affair with no out of school contextual significance whatsoever. Bilingual education that is left to the schools alone will have the same fate. The school can provide instructional power for bilingual education but not functional power for it. The latter must be provided by the community itself in terms of either dignifying its own diversity or (that of) the international community ... . If the unmarked language community is apathetic or opposed, and if all the interest in bilingual education comes from oppressed minorities, bilingual education finds itself in a context of pressures, tensions, grievances, conflicts, and cleavages.   (Wright, 1982, p.14)

APPENDIX B

Some Comparisons with Other Countries

1 USA legislation

The state of Massachusetts, USA, passed crucial legislation in November, 1971. The preamble declared:

> Section 1. Declaration of policy. The General Court finds that there are large numbers of children in the commonwealth who come from environments where the primary language is other than English. Experience has shown that public school classes in which instruction is given only in English are often inadequate for the education of children whose native tongue is another language. The General Court believes that a compensatory program of transitional bilingual education can meet the needs of these children and facilitate their integration into the regular public school curriculum. Therefore, pursuant to the policy of the commonwealth to ensure equal opportunity to every child, and in recognition of the needs of the children of limited English-speaking ability, it is the purpose of this act to provide for the establishment of transitional bilingual education programs in the public schools, and to provide supplemental financial assistance to help local school districts to meet the extra costs of such programs. (Massachusetts Board of Education, 1972)

This legislation gave a right to parents to elect a Parent Advisory Committee, declared a right for children of limited English-speaking ability to have tuition through the medium of their first language if there are "more than twenty ... of one language group" (op. cit., p3), protected "heritage language teaching", arranged for state funding, and established a bilingual bureau!

The historic 1974 USA Federal Government Court ruling led to the essential needs of bilingual pupils being embodied in legislation. The Court ruled importantly:

> There is no equality of treatment by providing students with the same facilities, teachers and curriculum. Students who do not understand English are effectively foreclosed from a meaningful education.
> (Lau vs. Nichols, 414 US.565, 1974)

In, for instance, Boston, USA, one can see the effect of formal policy, embodied in the School Board's firmly stated plan. This is an extract from their preamble:

> The Boston School Committee affirms its obligation to

assist children from distinct linguistic and cultural
backgrounds to realize these educational goals, while at
the same time enriching the entire school system by
sharing these linguistic and cultural backgrounds among
all members. It is therefore necessary and appropriate
that the Boston Public Schools continue to provide
bilingual/multilingual education programs which will
permit children to learn in more than one language and be
exposed to the distinct cultural heritages represented in
the Boston Public Schools. For this reason, educational
programs have been developed to provide instruction in
their native language so that limited English proficiency
children will receive a complete education, comparable to
that of other children; at the same time, they will
develop their English communication skills to a level
comparable with the skills of children whose native
language is English. These programs will continue to be
improved and expanded. Recognising the increased
educational value that learning and competency in more
than one language and exposure to different cultures have
in the attainment of its goals, the Boston School
Committee affirms its commitment to bilingual/multi-
cultural education programs.

(Boston Public Schools, 1984, p.3)

2   Subject learning in Sweden

Tuition in subjects is legally obligatory in the mother-tongue until
the pupil's Swedish is good enough, as the Swedish Government
describes in its Directive 5.

On 21 June 1979 the Government issued an Ordinance
Concerning Experimental Time Schedule Adjustments for Home
Language Instruction at the Junior and Intermediate Levels
of Compulsory School (SO-FS 1979:133). These experimental
activities are to comprise single-language preparatory
classes (otherwise termed home language classes) and other
arrangements, e.g. what are known as composite classes.
In single-language classes, children from one language
group only are taught their home language and given other
lessons in that language. Swedish is then successively
introduced as the teaching language. A concise report on
the experimental scheme is to be presented to the
Government by the NBE not later than 1 October 1982,
together with practical recommendations. The NBE
exercising powers conferred by the Ordinance, has issued
further regulations concerning the experimental activities
(SO-FS 1979:194). In addition to home language lessons,
home language study guidance and supportive Swedish
lessons, upper secondary school arrangements also include
special introductory courses and supplementary summer

courses for young immigrants.
(Ministry of Education and Cultural Affairs, Sweden, Immigrant Questions in the School System and Adult Education, Directive 1981:49, 1981:p.2.)

3   Subject learning in Bavaria

Phasing arrangements are fairly typical in Bavaria as the Bavarian Government report to the Commission of the European Communities makes clear:

Bilingual classes
These offer tuition from the 1st to 9th year of schooling using the mother-tongue as a medium of teaching with a gradual shift towards the use of German. One type of bilingual class has been in operation since 1973 and 1980 saw the introduction of another type better adapted to the needs of foreign pupils who already have some knowledge of German on entry into primary school.

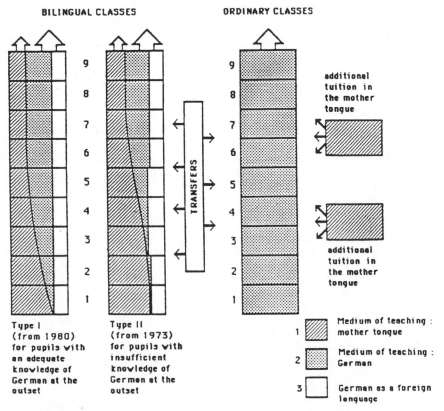

(Commission of the European Communities, 1984, p. DE(BA)2)

4   Australian E2L Organisation

Philosophy

a)   E2L Provision is argued and justified in terms of EQUALITY of
     access to mainstream culture and institutions.

b)   Bilingualism/multi-culturalism is argued in terms of HUMAN
     RIGHTS to retain and develop own language, culture, etc.

Organization of E2L

a)   New arrivals (age 4 - 18 or 19) are screened centrally by
     qualified   people,   and after assessment as beginners or
     otherwise in English,   are referred to Language Centres or
     Literacy Centres for beginners, or schools for later stage
     learners.

b)   Those assessed as beginners are entitled by Statute to full-
     time intensive course of up to 5 terms in a Language or
     Literacy Centre, where a full-ranging curriculum is attempted.

c)   Language/Literacy Centres have status of schools as far as
     enrolment is concerned.

d)   Centre Staff are involved with placement of their ex-pupils and
     with monitoring later progress in schools.

e)   (i) School staffing needs for E2L are assessed on a formula
          and funding is provided by national government.

     (ii) "Ethnic-aides" are funded and provided on a similar basis.

f)   In-School E2L teachers are concerned with

          (i)   small withdrawal groups of later stage learners.

          (ii) in-class support of bilingual learners.

          (iii) adaptation of materials to make them more accessible
                to bilingual pupils.

119

Bibliography and references

FOREWORD

Bourne, J (1987) Changing Perceptions, Changing Ways: The Initial Training of teachers of English as a Second Language in England ESOL Department, University of London Institute of Education.

Craft, M & Atkins, M (1983) Training Teachers of Ethnic Minority Community Languages Nottingham University School of Education. ISBN 0 85459 094 X

DES (1985) Education for All The Swann Report. HMSO ISBN 0 10 194530 2

Linguistic Minorities Project (1983) Linguistic Minorities in England ULIE and Heinemann Educational. ISBN 0 85473 165 2

Little, A & Willey, R (1983) Studies in the Multi-ethnic Curriculum Schools Council.

Townsend, H & Brittan, E (1972) Organisation in Multiracial Schools. ISBN 0 901225 88 6

Young, K & Connelly, N (1981) Policy and Practice in the Multi-racial City Policy Studies Institute. ISBN 0 85374 194 8

TOWARDS A CURRICULUM POLICY FOR A MULTILINGUAL WORLD

The main bulk of this bibliography is a study bibliography I prepared for my own use and for colleagues. It is of course not complete, and many of the books contain fuller bibliographies. However, I have found all these works of some help in thinking about the curriculum for a multilingual world and the education of bilingual learners, and those I have found especially useful I have marked with an asterisk. In addition, all references cited in the text of the report have been included.

M.M.

Bulman, Lesley (1984), Teaching Language and Study Skills in Secondary Science, Heinemann Educational Books. ISBN 0 435 57085 4

Burchfield, Robert (1985), The English Language, Oxford University Press. Centre for Information on Language Teaching (1976), Bilingualism and British Education: the dimensions of diversity, CILT.

Commission for Racial Equality (1980), The EEC's Directive on the Education of Children of Migrant Workers: Its implications for the education of children from ethnic minority groups in the UK, CRE.

Commission of the European Communities (1984), Final Report for the Commission to the Council on the Implementation of Directive 77/480/EEC on the Education of Migrant Workers, Brussels, CEC.

Committee of Enquiry, Chaired by Sir Alan Bullock (1975), A Language for Life, HMSO.

Committee of Enquiry, Chaired by Lord Swann (1985), Education for All, (The Swann Report). Department of Education and Science (1980), A Framework for the Curriculum, HMSO.

Department of Education and Science (1981), Directive of the Council of the European Community on the Education of the Children of Migrant Workers, Circular 5/81, 31 July 1981, DES and Welsh Office.

Department of Education and Science and Welsh Office (1982), Foreign Languages in the School Curriculum, A Consultation Paper, DES/Welsh Office.

Dolson, David P. (1985), "The Effects of Spanish Home Language Use
on the Scholastic Performance of Hispanic Pupils", in Journal
of Multilcultural and Multilingual Development, Vol. 6, No. 2,
1985. p.p.135-155 (includes a bibliography), ISSN 0143-4632.

European Economic Community (1977), council Directive, (77/486/EEC),
Official Journal of the European Communities.

#
Hawkins, Eric (1984), Awareness of Language: An Introduction,
Cambridge University Press. ISBN 0 521 28853 3

Hobbes, Thomas (1651), Leviathan.

Inner London Education Authority (1982), Bilingualism in the ILEA -
The Educational Implications of the 1981 Census, report
(25.6.82) by the Education Officer, ILEA 2321, ILEA.

ILEA Division-Two Working Party (1985), The Education of Bilingual
Learners, North Westminster Community School.

Ingham, Jennie (1983-5), various bilingual pupil texts, Middlesex
Polytechnic.

Joseph, Keith (1984), Secretary of State's Speech: EC Mother Tongue
Colloquium, Monday 26 March, 1984, DES.

Khan, Verity, (1985), Chapter Seven of the Swann Report, Institute
of Education, London University.

Klein, Gillian (1985), The School Library for Multi-cultural
Awareness, Educational Libraries Bulletin Special Supplement
23, University of London Institute of Education, Trentham
Books, ISBN 0 948080 03 5.

Lau v. Nichols (1974), United States Supreme Court Decision.

Linguistic Minorities Project (1985), The Other Languages of England
Routledge and Kegan Paul.

Little, Alan, and Willey, Richard (1981), Multi-Ethnic Education:
The Way Forward, Schools Council Pamphlet 18, Schools Council /
Longman. MacDonald, Barry, Adelman, Clem, Kushner, Saville,
and Walker, Rob (1982), Bread and Dreams: A case study of
bilingual schooling in the USA, Centre for Applied Research in
Education (CARE), University of East Anglia.

Marland, Michael (1977), "Subject Reading Strategies", in Marland,
Michael,(Ed.), Language Across the Curriculum, Heinemann
Educational Books. ISBN 0 435 80578 9

Marland, Michael (1978), "Responsibility for Reading in the
    Secondary School", in Chapman, L. John, and Czerniewska, Pan,
    Reading: From Process to Practice, Routledge and Kegan Paul in
    association with the Open University Press. ISBN 0 7100 00553

Marland, Michael (1980), The Teaching of Non-European Languages,
    North Westminster Community School.

Marland, Michael, and Goodhand, Laurie, (1985) "Pastoral Care for
    Bilingual Students", in Pastoral Care, Volume 3, Number 3,
    November 1985, Basil Blackwell (reprinted from ILEA Division
    Two, 1985, op. cit.).

Mother Tongue and English Teaching Project (Motet) (n.d.), Summary
    of the Report - Vols.I and II, School of Research in Education,
    University of Bradford.

Pomphrey, Cathy (1985), Language Varieties and Change, Cambridge
    University Press. ISBN 0 521 28849 5

Schools Council Modern Languages Committee (1982), The Second
    Foreign Language in Secondary Schools: A Question of Survival,
    Schools Council.

Srivastava, Satyendra (1982), "The Teaching of Asian Languages in
    Secondary Schools", in Contemporary Review, vol.240, No.1394,
    March, 1982.

Tansley, Paula and Craft, Alma (1984), "Mother Tongue Teaching and
    Support: A Schools Council Enquiry", in Journal of Multilingual
    and Multicultural Development, Vol.5, No.5, 1984, Multilingual
    Matters Ltd.

Part II

THE EDUCATION OF BILINGUAL LEARNERS

Baetens Beardsmore, Hugo, 1982, Bilingualism: Basic Principles,
Multilingual Matters, Tieto, ISBN 0 905028 04 X, (PBK), ISBN 0
905028 05 8.

Bahtnagar, Joti, (ed.) 1981, Educating Immigrants, Croom Helm,
ISBN 0 7099 0310 3.

Boye-Moller, Monica, September 1982, A Review of Immigrant
Education in Sweden, No.292, Swedish Institute, Box 7434, S-
103 91 Stockholm, Sweden.

Braithwaite, Edward Kamu,1984, History of the Voice: The
Development of National Language in Anglophone Caribbean
Poetry, New Beacon Books, ISBN 0 901241 55 5.

Broadbent, J. et al.,1983, Assessment in a Multicultural Society:
Community Languages at 16+, Longman Resources Unit.
ISBN 0 582 38940 2

Broadbent, John, 1984, "Modern Languages", in Craft, Alma, and
Bardell, Geoff (Eds.), Curriculum Opportunities in a
Multicultural Society, Harper and Row, ISBN 0 06 318285 8.

Brown, M. Daphne, 1979, Mother tongue to English: The young child
in the multicultural school, Cambridge University Press,
ISBN 0521 21873 X ISBN (paperback) 0 521 29299 9.

Bullock Report, - see Committee of Enquiry, 1975,A Language for
life..... Bulman, Lesley, 1984, Teaching Language and Study
Skills in Secondary Science, Heinemann Educational Books.

Burchfield, Robert, 1985, The English Language, Oxford University
Press. Centre for Information on Language Teaching (1976),
Bilingualism and British Education: the dimensions of
diversity, CILT. ISBN 0 19 219173 X

Candlin, Christopher, and Derrick, June, January 1972, Technical
Monographs 2: Language, Community Relations Commission.

Central Advisory Council for Education (England), 1963, Half Our
Future, Report of the Council chaired by John Newsom, HMSO.

Central Advisory Council for Education (England), 1967, Children
and Their Primary Schools, Volume 1: Report, report of the
Council chaired by Lady Plowden, HMSO.

Centre for Information on Language Teaching and Research, 1975, Less Commonly Taught Languages: Resources and Problems, papers from a conference convened in June 1975, CILT, ISBN 0 903466 08 2.

* Centre for Information on Language Teaching and Research, 1976, Bilingualism and British Education: The Dimensions of Diversity, papers from a conference convened in January, 1976, CILT, ISBN 0 903466 10 4.

* Cohen, Gaynor, 1984, The Politics of Bilingual Education, Oxford Review of Education, Volume 10, No.2, pp. 225-239.

Commission for Racial Equality, 1980, A Tower of Babel?! Mother Tongues?, CRE.

* Commission for Racial Equality, 1980, The EEC's Directive on the Education of Children of Migrant Workers: Its implications for the education of children from ethnic minority groups in the UK, CRE.

* Commission for Racial Equality, 1982, Ethnic Minority Community Languages: A Statement, CRE.

Commission for Racial Equality, 1982, Day Consultation with Part-Time Mother-Tongue Classes, Fourth, Greater London, CRE.

* Commission of the European Communities COM(84) 54, 10 February 1984, Final Report from the Commission to the Council on the implementation of Directive 77/486/EEC on the education of the children of migrant workers, Brussels, CEC.

* Commission on Migrants' Languages and Culture in Sweden, 1984, English Summary from the Main Report 'Different Origins - Partnership in Sweden, Education for Linguistic and Cultural Diversity' (SOU 1983:57), Utbildings-Depertementet, Regering-skansliets Offsetcentral, Stockholm, ISBN 91 38 08139 3.

Committee of Enquiry appointed by the Secretary of State for Education and Science under the Chairmanship of Sir Alan Bullock F.B.A., 1975, A Language for Life, (Bullock Report), HMSO, ISBN 0 11 270326 7.

Committee of Enquiry, Chaired by Lord Swann, 1985, Education for All, (The Swann Report). Department of Education and Science (1980), A Framework for the Curriculum, HMSO. ISBN 0 10 194530 2

Committee on the Curriculum and Organisation of Secondary Schools, 1984, Improving Secondary Schools, Report of the Committee chaired by David Hargreaves, ILEA.

Community Relations Commission, Candlin, Christopher, and Derrick, June, January 1972, Technical Monographs 2: Language, CRC.

Community Relations Commission, n.d., Evidence from the Community Relations Commission to the Select Committee on Race Relations and Immigration.

Community Relations Commission, n.d. Evidence from the Community Relations Commission to the Committee of Enquiry into Reading and the Use of English.

Community Relations Commission, 1972, Training Teachers for a Multi-Cultural Society, Report of a conference for lecturers in Colleges and Depts. of Education, organised by the Community Relations Commission at Nottingham College of Education, 5 - 8 September 1972.

Corner, Trevor, (Ed.), 1984, Education in Multi-Cultural Societies, Croom Helm for the British Comparative and International Education Society. ISBN 0 7099 3407 6

Craft, Alma, and Bardell, Geoffrey (Eds.), 1984, Curriculum Opportunities in a Multicultural Society, Harper and Row, ISBN 0 06 318285 8.

* Cummins, Jim (ed.), June 1981, Heritage Language Education: Issues and Directions, Ontario Institute for Studies in Education, Proceedings of a Conference organised by the Multiculturalism Directorate of the Department of the Secretary of State, Saskatoon, ISBN 0 662 12426 X.

Cummins, Jim, 1983, "Language Proficiency, Biliteracy and French Immersion", Canadian Journal of Education, 8 (2), pp 117-138.

Cummins, Jim, January 1983, Heritage Language Programs: A Literature Review, Ontario Institute for Studies in Education, A literature review funded under contract by the Ministry of Education, Ontario.

Cummins, Jim, n.d., Bilingualism and Minority Language Children, Modern Language Centre, Ontario Institute for Studies in Education.

126

Cummins, Jim, 1984, a chapter, in Rivera, Charlene (Ed.), Language Proficiency and Academic Achievement, No.10 in the series Multilingual Matters, MM Productions.

Dawe, Lloyd, n.d., The Influence of a Child's First Language on Reasoning in Mathematics, University of Cambridge.

Department of Education and Science, 1981, Directive of the Council of the European Community on the Education of the Chidren of Migrant Workers, Circular 5/81, 31 July, 1981, DES and Welsh Office.

Department of Education and Science and Welsh Office, 1982, Foreign Languages in the School Curriculum, A Consultation Paper Department of Education and Science/Welsh Office.

Derrick, June, 1966, Teaching English to Immigrants, Longman, ISBN 0 582 54002 X.

Dickinson, L., Hobbs, A., Kleinberg, S.M., Martin, P.J., 1975, Jordanhill College of Education, The Immigrant School Learner: A study of Pakistani Pupils in Glasgow, NFER, ISBN 85633 062 0.

Dillard, J.L., 1973, Black English: Its History and Usage in the United States, Vintage Books, ISBN 0 394 71872 0.

Dolson, David P., 1985, "The effects of Spanish Home Language Use on the Scholastic performance of Hispanic Pupils", in Journal of Multicultural and Multilingual Development, Vol.6, No.2, 1985. pp 135-155 (includes a bibliography), ISSN 0143-4632.

Donmall, B.G., 1985, Language Awareness, CILT, ISBN 0 903466 996

Donmall, B.G., 1986, Education (No. 2), S Act, HMSO. ISBN 0 546 1865

Edwards, V.K., 1979, The West Indian Language Issue in British Schools: Challenges and Responses, Routledge & Kegan Paul, ISBN 0 7100 0172 X, ISBN 0 7100 0173 8 (pbk).

European Economic Community, 1977, Council Directive, (77/486/EEC), Official Journal of the European Communities.

Fishman, J.A., 1976, Bilingual Education - An International Sociolinguistic Perspective, Newbury House, ISBN 0 88377 056 3.

Glyn Lewis, E., 1981, Bilingualism and Bilingual Education, Pergamon Press, ISBN 0 08 025326 1.

Gorman, T.P., 1982, Observations on "The ILEA Perspective" by Peter Newsam, paper at BAAL Conference on Language and Ethnicity, available from NFER.

Gorman, T.P., White, J., Orchard, J., and Tate, A., 1982, Language Performance in Schools, Department of Education and Science Welsh Office, Department of Education for Northern Ireland, Assessment of Performance Unit, HMSO, ISBN 0 11 270387 9.

Hargreaves Committee - see Committee on the Curriculum and Organisation of Secondary Schools.

* Hawkins, Eric, 1984, Awareness of Language : An Introduction, Cambridge University Press, ISBN 0 521 28853 3

HMI, 1984, Mother Tongue Teaching in School and Community, an HMI Enquiry in Four LEAs, HMSO.

Hobbes, Thomas, 1651, Leviathan.

Home Affairs Committee, 20 July 1981, Fifth Report Session 1980-81, Racial Disadvantage, Volume 1, House of Commons, HC 424-1, HMSO.

Home Affairs Committee, January 1982, Racial Disadvantage, The Government Reply to the Fifth Report from the Home Affairs Committee Session 1980-1981, HC 424, HMSO, Cmnd. 8476, ISBN 0 10 184760 2.

* Houlton, David, and Willey, Richard, 1983, Supporting Children's Bilingualism, some Policy Issues for Primary Schools and Education Authorities, Longman for the schools Council, ISBN 0 582 38901 1.

ILEA, 1973, An Education Service for the Whole Community, ILEA.

ILEA, 1981, Learning Materials Service, Education in a Multi-ethnic Society, An aide-memoire for the Inspectorate, ILEA.

ILEA, 1982, Bilingualism in the ILEA - The Educational Implications of the 1981 Language Census, report (25.6.82), by the Education Officer, ILEA 2321.

ILEA, 1982, Research and Statistics, Catalogue of Languages Spoken by ILEA School Pupils, ILEA, RS 838/82.

ILEA, 1983, Race, Sex and Class, 2. Multi-Ethnic Education in Schools, ILEA.

* ILEA, Research and Statistics, 1983, 1983 Language Census, RS 916/83, ILEA.

* ILEA, 1984, English as a Second Language Courses and Classes for Young People aged 16 to 19, Division 2: Camden and Westminster, ILEA, 1984-85.

Ingham, Jennie, (series editor) Dual Language Story Books from the Reading Materials for Minority Groups Project, at Middlesex Polytechnic, available from Baker Book Services, Little Mead, Alford Road, Cranleigh, Surrey GU6 8NU.

Issues Collective, Summer 1983, "Learning and Language, ESL in the mainstream classroom", Issues in Race and Education, No. 39 ISSN 0308 3233.

Jeffcoate, Robert, 1984, Ethnic Minorities and Education, Harper and Row, ISBN 0 06 318284 X.

Joseph, Sir Keith, "Speech to the EEC Mother-Tongue Colloquium", Monday, 26 March, 1984, DES.

Khan, Verity, 1985, Chapter Seven of the Swann Report, Institute of Education, London University.

Klein, Gillian, 1985, The School Library for Multi-cultural Awareness, Education Libraries Bulletin Special Supplement 23, University of London Institute of Education, Trentham Books, ISBN 0 948080 03 5.

Kringas, Paul, and Lewins, Frank, 1981, Why Ethnic Schools? Selected Case Studies, Australian National University Press, Canberra, ISBN 0 7081 0367 7.

Le Page, R., and Tabouret-Keller, A., 1982, "Models and Stereotypes of Ethnicity and Language" Journal of Multilingual and Multicultural Development, Vol. 3, No.3, Multilingual Matters, ISSN 0143 4632.

Lambert, W.E., 1977, "The effect of bilingualism on the individual: cognitive and sociocultural consequences", in Hornby, P.A. (Ed.), Bilingualism: Psychological, Social and Educational Implications, New York, Academic Press.

Lau v. Nichols, 1974, United States Supreme Court Decision.

Linguistic Minorities in England, A report by the Linguistic
Minorities Project for the Department of Education and
Science, July 1983, University of London Institute of
Education, ISBN 0 85473 165 2.

* Linguistic Minorities in England, A Short Report on the
Linguistic Minorities Project, September 1983, University of
London Institute of Education. ISBN 0 85473 165 2

Linguistic Minority Project, 1985, The Other Languages of
England, Routledge and Kegan Paul, ISBN 0 7100 999290,
(Paperback) ISBN 0 7102 04175.

Little, Alan, and Willey, Richard, 1981, Multi-Ethnic Education:
The Way Forward, Schools Council Pamphlet 18, Schools
Council/Longman.

Macbeth, Alastair, 1984, The Child Between, a Report on School-
Family Relations in the Countries of the European Community,
The Office of the European Communities. ISBN 92 825 4382 X

* MacDonald, Barry, Adelman, Clem, Kushner, Saville, and Walker,
Rob. October 1982, Bread and Dreams: A case study of
bilingual schooling in the U.S.A., Centre for Applied
Research in Education (CARE), University of East Anglia, ISBN
0 904510 10 7.

Marland, Michael, 1977, "Subject Reading Strategies", in Marland,
Michael, (Ed.), Languages Across the Curriculum, Heinemann
Educational Books. 0 435 80578 9

Marland, Michael, 1978, "Responsibility for Reading in the
Secondary School", in Chapman, L. John, and Czerniewska, Pam,
Reading: From Process to Practice,Routledge and Kegan Paul in
association with the Open University Press. ISBN 0 7100 00553

Marland, Michael, 1980, Non-European Languages and the
Curriculum, North Westminster Community School, London.

Mayer, Lynne, February 1983, A Pregnant Pause? Communication
between women whose first language is not English and
antenatal clinics in Paddington and North Kensington,
Paddington and North Kensington Community Health Council.

Milner, David, 1983, Children and Race Ten Years On, Ward Lock
Educational, ISBN 0 7062 4268 8.

Milroy, L., 1982, "Language and Group Identity", Journal of
Multilingual and Multicultural Development, Vol.3, No.3,
Multilingual Matters, ISSN 0143 4632.

Mother Tongue and English Teaching Project (Motet), n.d., Summary
of the Report - Vols.I and II, School of Research in
Education, University of Bradford.

National Congress on Languages in Education, 1982, Report on
Working Party on The Languages of Minority Communities, NCLE.
See Reid, E.

National Congress on Languages in Education, 1984, Language
Awareness, see Donmall, B.G.

National Council for Mother Tongue Teaching (NCMTT), Aims,
available from NCMTT, Little Place, Hollyhock Lane, New St.,
Painswick, Glos., G66 6XH.

National Swedish Board of Education, Information Section, n.d.,
Home Language, S-106 42 Stockholm.

National Swedish Board of Education, Information Section, October
1978, Swedish For Adult Immigrants, S-106 42 Stockholm.

National Swedish Board of Education, Information Section,
October 1979, Local Experience of Experimental
Introductory Courses And Supplementary Summer Courses For
Young Immigrants Attending Upper Secondary School,
S-106 42 Stockholm.

National Swedish Board of Education, Information Section, March
1978, Pupils With A Home Language Other Than Swedish Or With
A Non-Swedish Cultural Back-Ground, S-106 42 Stockholm.

National Swedish Board of Education, Information Section,
February 1979, Immigrant Instruction As A Part Of Municipal
Adult Education And Basic Education For Adults, S-106 42
Stockholm.

National Swedish Board of Education, Information Section,
February 1979, Immigrant Education Provided by Adult
Education Associations and Folk High Schools, S-106 42
Stockholm.

National Swedish Board of Education, Information Section, May
1979, Organisation and Planning for Home Language
Instruction and Auxiliary Swedish Lessons in Compulsory
School S-106 42 Stockholm.

National Swedish Board of Education, Information Section,
November 1979, Special Labour Market Training Measures On
Behalf Of Immigrants, S-106 42 Stockholm.

National Swedish Board of Education, Information Section, 1979, There Have Always Been Immigrants in Stockholm, S-106 42 Stockholm.

National Swedish Board of Education, Information Section, April 1980, Service Material for The Home Language Instruction of Greek in the 9-Year Compulsory School, Compiled at the National Board of Education by a Study group from the Stockholm School of Education, S-106 42, Stockholm.

National Swedish Board of Education, Information Section, January 1981, Compulsory School Leavers in 1979 with Home Languages Other Than Swedish, S-106 42 Stockholm, Interim Report 1.

National Swedish Board of Education, Information Section, July 1981, Compulsory School Leavers in 1979 with Home Languages Other Than Swedish, S-106 42 Stockholm, Interim Report 2.

National Swedish Board of Education, Information Section, September 1981, Compulsory School Leavers in 1979 with Home Languages Other Than Swedish, S-106 42 Stockholm, Interim Report 3.

Newsom Report - see Central Advisory Council for Education (England), 1963.

Plowden Report - see Central Advisory Council for Education (England), 1967.

Pomphrey, Cathy, 1985, Language Varieties and Change, Cambridge University Press. ISBN 0 521 28849 5

Price, Erwen, 1978, Bilingual Education in Wales 5 - 11, report of the Schools Council Bilingual Education Project 1968-77, Evans/Methuen Educational, ISBN 0 423 50520 3.

Pyle, Aline, 1980, "The Case for Teaching Asian Languages in School", MS education course essay, quoted in Marland, 1980, op. cit..

* Reid, Euan, (ed.), Minority Community Languages in School, 1984, NCLE Papers and Reports 4, Centre for Information on Language Teaching and Research, ISBN 0 903466 70 8.

Richmond, John, (Vauxhall Manor School), 1976-77, Dialect, Some aspects of dialect in children's writing, English Centre.

Rosen, Harold, and Burgess, Tony, 1980, Languages and Dialects of London School Children, An Investigation, Ward Lock, ISBN 0 7062 40871.

Saville-Troike, Muriel, 1976, Foundations for Teaching English as a Second Language, Theory and method for multicultural education, Prentice Hall Inc. ISBN 0 13 329946 5.

Schools Council Working Paper 31, 1970, Immigrant Children in Infant Schools, Schools Council, ISBN 423 44990 7.

Schools Council Mother Tongue Project, 26-29 March 1984, Report to the European Community Colloquium, Schools Council.

Schools Council Modern Languages Committee, Spring 1982, The Second Foreign Language in Secondary Schools: A Question of Survival, Schools Council Occasional Bulletins from the Subject Committees.

Schools Council, 1978, Scope, Handbook 3, English for Immigrant Children in the Infant School, Schools Council Project in English for Immigrant Children, Schools Council, Longman, ISBN 0 582 09180 2.

Secretaries of State for Education in England and Wales, 1980, A Framework for the School Curriculum, DES.

Select Committee on Race Relations and Immigration, Session 1972-73, 24 July 1973, Education, Volume 1, Report, House of Commons, HC 40 5-1, HMSO.

Select Committee on Race Relations and Immigration, Session 1976-77, February 1977, The West Indian Community, Volume 1, House of Commons, HC 180-1, HMSO.

Spillane, Robert R., January 1984, School Profiles Boston Public Schools 1982-1983, A Report of The Boston Public Schools to the Community.

Spolsky, Bernard, and Cooper, Robert, L. Robert, (Editors), 1978, Case Studies in Bilingual Education, Newbury House, USA.

* Srivestava, Satyendra, March 1982, "The Teaching of Asian Languages in Secondary Schools", Contemporary Review, Vol. 240, No. 1394, March 1982, London.

Sutcliffe, David, 1982, British Black English, Basil Blackwell, ISBN 0 631 12711 9.

Swain, Merrill, and Lapkin, Sharon, n.d., Evaluating Bilingual Education: A Canadian Case Study, Multilingual Matters 2, ISBN 0 905028 10 4, ISBN 0 905028 09 0 (Paperback).

Tansley, Paula, and Craft, Alma, 1984, "Mother Tongue Teaching and Support : A Schools Council Enquiry", in Journal of Multilingual and Multicultural Development, Vol. 5, No.5, Multicultural Matters Limited.

Tillander -, Swedish Minister of Education and Cultural Affairs, Immigrant Questions in the School System and Adult Education, Swedish Government, Dir 1981:49.

Tomlinson, Sally, 1983, Ethnic Minorities in British Schools, A review of the literature, 1960-1982, Policy Studies Institute, Heinemann Educational Books, ISBN 0 435 83937 3, (paperback) ISBN 0 435 83938 1.

University of Cambridge, Department of Education, Teaching Mathematics through English as a Second Language, Seminar held at Department of Education, University of Cambridge, 4th December 1982.

Wallis, Susan, November 1977, Bengali Families in Camden, a report on the Community Health Project of the Camden Committee for Community Relations, Camden Committee for Community Relations.

Willey, Richard, 1982, Teaching in Multicultural Britain, Schools Council Programme 4, Individual Pupils, Longman for Schools Council. ISBN 0 582 39680 8

* Wright, John, 1982, Bilingualism in Education, Issues in Race and Education, 11 Carleton Gardens, Brecknock Road, London N19 5AQ.

Journals

Multicultural Teaching. Editor: Gillian Klein, Trentham Books Ltd., 30 Wenger Crescent, Trentham, Stoke-on-Trent, Staff. ST4 8LE.

The Bilingual Family Newsletter. Editor: George Saunders, Bank House, 8a Hill Road, Clevedon, Avon BS21 7HH.

Other CILT publications

Towards intercultural education
U Boos-Nünning, M Hohmann, H H Reich, F Wittek
A comparative study of the education of migrant children in Belgium, England, France and the Netherlands. The book provides a critical assessment of the pilot projects mounted in these countries and draws up recommendations for the further development of reception teaching and mother tongue teaching. The book concludes with proposals for intercultural education.
A5 Paperback 240pp 1986 ISBN O 948003 36 7

Teaching Britain's community languages: materials and methods
By Marion Molteno
This book will help the practising teacher to select and provide suitable materials for the widely varying needs of the learners. The examples are taken from Urdu, but the problems discussed are common to the teaching of most community languages in Britain. Among the broad topics are: the learners and their needs; experimenting with new methods; new books for secondary schools; designing a course book.
A5 Paperback 112pp 1986 ISBN O 948003 65 0

Britain's South Asian languages
By Michael Mobbs
An introduction to the principal languages spoken by people of South Asian origin living in Britain. The four chapters cover: the Indo-European connection; linguistic background and characteristics; socio-historical background and present-day status; South Asian languages in the British context.
A5 Paperback 56pp 1985 ISBN O 903466 99 6

English as a second language: sources and resources
Compiled and edited by June Geach
A guide for teachers of English to children and adults who are resident in Britain but do not speak English as a mother tongue. Contents include: details of relevant organisations and associations; periodicals; selected annotated list of relevant published works; activities and services of teachers' centres in the ESL/CL/multicultural field.
A5 Paperback 80pp 1986 ISBN O 948003 75 8

Language and Culture Guides
A series of 28 guides to less commonly taught languages, such as **Arabic**, **Chinese**, **Gujarati**, **Hindi**, **Japanese**, **Urdu**, and others. Each title gives detailed information on the provision and use of language teaching and learning resources.

For details of all CILT publications write to:
Centre for Information on Language Teaching and Research
Regent's College, Inner Circle, Regent's Park, London NW1 4NS